Making Gifts in Counted Cross-Stitch

PROJECT IDEAS
AND OVER ONE HUNDRED
CHARTED DESIGNS

Jana Hauschild

BLANDFORD

MAKING GIFTS IN COUNTED CROSS STITCH.
Volume form: copyright © Blandford Press,
London 1990
Text: copyright © Jana Hauschild Lindberg 1990

**Library of Congress Cataloging-in-Publication
Data**

Hauschild, Jana.
    Making gifts in counted cross stitch / Jana
Hauschild; translated with an introduction by
Linda Seward
        p.   cm.
    ISBN 0-312-05216-2
    1. Cross-stitch--Patterns.   I. Title.
TT778.C76L565 1991
746.44'3041--dc20   90-37311
                                                       CIP

            ISBN 0-312-05216-2 (pbk.)
            ISBN 0-312-05227-8 (hbk.)

First published in Great Britain by Blandford Press

            First U.S. edition
            10 9 8 7 6 5 4 3 2 1

Typeset by Litho Link Ltd., Welshpool, Powys, Wales
Printed and bound in Yugoslavia by Papirografika

· MAKING GIFTS IN ·

COUNTED CROSS-STITCH

Dozens of project ideas, including motifs, borders and more than 100 charted designs

JANA HAUSCHILD

St. Martin's Press
New York

·Contents·

3. BORDER DESIGNS

4. ROUND DESIGNS

5. SQUARED, RECTANGULAR AND ALLOVER DESIGNS

6. LARGE DESIGNS

·1·

Counted Cross-Stitch
Technique and Projects

Counted cross-stitch is one of the simplest forms of embroidery. It consists of a series of crossed stitches embroidered on an evenweave fabric over the intersection of the horizontal and vertical threads. The stitches are worked following a chart. Each cross-stitch is indicated by a symbol; the different symbols represent different colours (Fig.1). You can work up the design as directed in the colour key, or make up your own original colour scheme.

Fig. 1

Candle		
⊙	972	light orange
⊠	606	dark orange-red
◣	310	black
–	310	black (backstitch)

The size of a cross-stitch design is determined by the type of fabric upon which it is embroidered. Although finished sizes for the designs are given in this book, it is easy to calculate

what a different finished size will be by using the following formula:

$$\frac{\text{Finished}}{\text{size}} = \frac{\text{Number of stitches}}{\text{Thread-count of fabric}}$$

For example, let's say you have selected a design that is 42 stitches wide and 98 stitches long and you would like to work on a cloth that has 5½ threads per cm/ 14 threads per inch. The finished width of your design can be determined by dividing the number of stitches (42) by the number of threads (5½/14), which gives you a design that is 7½ cm/3 inches wide. For the length, divide the number of stitches (98) by the thread count (5½/14) to find out that the design will be 17½ cm/7 inches long. If you feel this size is too large, try switching to a linen cloth, which has 10 threads per cm/25 threads per inch. The size in that case would be approximately 4 cm/1½ inches wide by 10 cm/4 inches long. Use this formula to decide quickly which thread count of fabric is best for you to use.

MATERIALS
Fabric
You can use any evenweave fabric made from cotton, linen, wool or synthetic blends. Cotton

and linen fabrics are the most widely used. Counted thread fabrics specially woven for cross-stitch, such as Aida or Hardanger, are available in many needlecraft shops, although these are limited in colour range. Aida fabric is cotton and can be bought in three sizes: 4½, 5½ or 7 threads per cm/11, 14 or 18 threads per inch. Hardanger cloth is available in linen or cotton. If you would like to embroider on an unusually-coloured fabric, try using linen which is available in most fabric shops. When using linen, one has to take into account the inevitable slubs and inconsistencies that occur in the weave; this is why it is best to work counted cross-stitch over two or more threads on linen fabric (*see* Fig.7). Thirty-count linen will give much the same effect as working on 14-count Aida cloth.

The materials used for the designs given in this book include linen and Aida. Linen measures are in threads, Aida measures are in stitches. Please note the following:

10 threads per cm = 25 per in.
8 threads per cm = 20 per in.
6 threads per cm = 15 per in.

5½ stitches per cm = 13½ per in.
4½ stitches per cm = 11 per in.

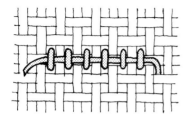

Fig. 2

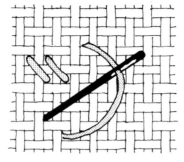

Fig. 3

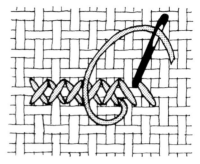

Fig. 4

Threads and yarns

Six-strand cotton embroidery floss is ideal for counted cross-stitch because the floss can be separated into the exact number of strands that provide the correct amount of coverage. Use thread or yarn that is the same thickness as the threads on the fabric you are embroidering. For flatter designs, separate the strands of floss and work with two strands of thread in your needle. If you wish to create a more textured effect, use more strands. You can also use silk or metallic threads, Danish Flower Thread, pearl cotton, even crewel wool, depending on the thread count of your fabric. To add some sparkle to a design, mix one strand of metallic thread with two strands of embroidery floss. Throughout this book I have referred to DMC six-strand embroidery floss. A conversion chart at the end of this chapter shows at a glance where you can make substitutions with flosses manufactured by two other companies: Royal Mouliné, or Bates/Anchor.

EQUIPMENT

Needles

Use a small blunt tapestry needle, size number 24 or 26, to prevent splitting the fabric threads.

Hoop

Work with a small round embroidery hoop which consists of an inner ring and an adjustable outer ring that tightens by turning a screw.

Scissors

You must have a pair of small sharp embroidery scissors for cutting threads and a pair of sharp fabric shears for cutting out the fabric.

TECHNIQUE

Depending upon the gift project that you would like to make (*see* instructions at the end of this chapter), cut out your fabric to the desired size plus about 2.5 cm/1 in around each of the edges. Overcast the edges of the fabric to prevent ravelling by hemming, zigzagging on the sewing machine or whipstitching. Find the centre of the fabric by folding it in half crosswise and lengthwise; mark the centre point with a small stitch. Then find the centre of your design (usually indicated on the charts by arrows). Do not begin your design at the centre; instead, count the number of squares on the chart from the centre point to the top, then count the same number of squares to the top of your fabric and work your first stitch there. Work the design in horizontal rows of colour from left to right.

Place the fabric in the embroidery hoop so that it is taut. Adjust the tension as you work so that the fabric is always firmly taut.

Begin stitching by leaving a length of waste thread on the back of the work, securing it with your first few stitches. Fig. 2 shows how the waste thread is secured on the wrong side of the work. Insert your needle into the holes of the fabric, working one slanted stitch over the intersection of two threads from lower right to upper left as shown in Fig.3. Continue working the required number of slanting stitches across the row, following the symbols on the chart. Then work back across the row, making slanting stitches from lower left to upper right finishing each cross-stitch as shown in Fig.4. (In Denmark and America, stitches are worked from lower left to upper right, then crossed from lower right to upper left. It makes no difference which way you stitch, as long as all the stitches are crossed in the same direction.)

When you are working a vertical row of stitches, cross each stitch in turn as shown in Fig.5. To end a line of stitching, finish your last stitch and keep the needle and thread on the wrong side of the work. Wiggle

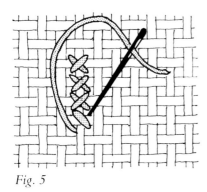

Fig. 5

the point of the needle beneath a few threads on the wrong side and pull the thread through as shown in Fig.6; clip off the excess thread so that the ends will not show through on the right side of the work.

If you are working on linen, or if you wish to make larger stitches, work over two sets of threads in each direction as shown in Fig.7. Your first few stitches may be difficult, but once you have established a row of stitches, you'll have no trouble counting two threads instead of one.

Backstitch

Backstitch is very commonly used in conjunction with counted cross-stitch to outline, delineate features or emphasize a portion of the design. Work the backstitches from one hole to the next in a horizontal, vertical or diagonal direction; *see* Fig.8.

Working with waste canvas

Counted cross-stitch can be worked on non-evenweave fabrics by using a non-interlock waste canvas. Select a canvas with a stitch count of the desired size. Cut the canvas slightly larger than the finished size of your design. Baste the canvas to your chosen fabric in the area you wish to embroider. Using a crewel or chenille needle, work the design over the canvas. As you work, stick the needle straight up and down through the fabric and canvas; take great care not to catch the canvas threads in your embroidery. When the embroidery is finished, remove the basting and dampen the canvas thoroughly using a warm wet towel. Gently pull out the canvas threads one by one; *see* p.42. Press the finished embroidery.

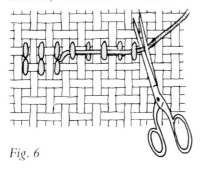

Fig. 6

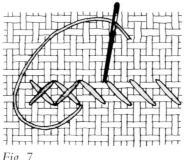

Fig. 7

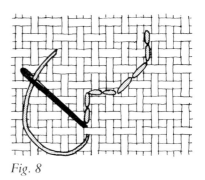

Fig. 8

• SMALL QUICK PROJECTS •

BOOKMARK

Cut piece of evenweave fabric about 15 × 5 cm/6 × 2 in. Overcast the raw edges. Embroider a small motif or border design on the fabric; gently press the finished embroidery. Trim away the overcast edge. Carefully draw away threads from the cut edges, creating a 6 mm/¼ in fringe.

GIFT TAG, PLACECARD or NAME LABEL

Cut evenweave fabric 2.5 cm/1 in larger than desired finished size. Overcast the raw edges. Embroider a small motif on the fabric; gently press the finished embroidery. Cut away excess fabric, leaving about 13 mm/½ in all around the edge of the design. Carefully draw away threads from the cut edges, creating a

6 mm/¼ in fringe. Glue the wrong side of the design to a rectangular piece of card. (*see* p.47)

PINCUSHION or SACHET

Cut evenweave fabric about 2.5 cm/1 in larger than desired finished size (or more, depending upon the size of the design). Overcast the raw edges. Embroider a small motif on the fabric; gently press the finished embroidery. Cut away excess fabric to desired size. Cut a matching piece of fabric for the back; stitch together with right sides facing and raw edges even, making a 6 mm/¼ in seam and leaving an opening for turning. Turn to the right side and stuff with kapok, fibrefill or potpourri until plump. Fold raw edges at opening inside and slipstich opening closed. (*see* p.25)

MATCHBOX COVER

Embroider a small motif on a piece of evenweave fabric; gently press the finished embroidery. Cut away excess fabric to the exact size of the matchbox you wish to decorate. Glue the wrong side of the design to the top of the matchbox, making sure the raw edges are securely glued so they do not unravel. (*see* p.34/35)

POCKET

Using a commercial pocket pattern, cut one pocket from evenweave fabric, adding the appropriate seam allowances. Embroider a small motif in the centre of the fabric; gently press the finished embroidery. Cut a matching piece of fabric for the lining; stitch together with right sides facing, leaving an opening for turning. Turn to the right side, fold raw edges at the opening inside, and slipstitch the opening closed. Press carefully. Topstitch the edges of the pocket if desired, then sew to the front of a blouse or skirt with small slipstitches.

TIE or COLLAR

Read the previous instructions for working with waste canvas. Select a small design. Centre the waste canvas on a tie or collar and baste into place. Work the design over the canvas, then remove the canvas threads as directed. Press the finished embroidery gently. (*see* p.36,46)

HANDKERCHIEF

Read the previous instructions for working with waste canvas. Select a small design. Position the waste canvas in the corner of a handkerchief and baste in place. Work the design over the canvas, then remove the canvas threads as directed. Press the finished embroidery gently. (*see* p.36)

T-SHIRT

Read the previous instructions for working with waste canvas. Select a medium to large-size design. Centre the waste canvas on the front of a T-shirt and baste in place. Work the design over the canvas, then remove the canvas threads as directed. Press the finished embroidery gently. (*see* p.15)

BABY'S BIB

Use the full-size pattern to cut a piece of evenweave fabric, adding 6 mm/¼ in all around. Overcast the raw edges. Find the centre of the bib at the neckline; begin working a small design about 2.5 cm/1 in below the raw neck edge or in the exact centre of the bib front. Gently press the finished embroidery. Trim away overcast edge. Finish the raw edges of the bib with bias binding, leaving excess binding at the back for tying. (*see* p.31,39)

CHRISTMAS ORNAMENTS

Cut evenweave fabric about 2.5 cm/1 in larger than desired finished size. Overcast the raw edges. Embroider a small motif on the fabric; gently press the finished embroidery. Cut away excess fabric to desired size; for a special effect, cut around the shape of the design, leaving a 6 mm/¼ in seam allowance all around. Cut a matching piece of fabric for the back; stitch together with right sides facing and raw edges even, making a 6 mm/¼ in seam and leaving an opening for turning. Clip any curved edges. Turn to the right side and stuff with kapok or polyester fibrefill until plump. Fold raw edges at opening inside and slipstitch opening closed.

• *DECORATING THE HOME* •

WALLHANGING

Calculate the finished size of your design using the formula on page 6; cut evenweave fabric 5 cm/ 2 in larger than the calculated size all around. Overcast the raw edges. Find the exact centre of the fabric and the design and count up to the top of the design and fabric. Begin embroidering downward until the design is finished. Carefully press the finished embroidery. Measure 3.8 cm/1½ in from the outer edge of the embroidery at the sides and bottom and trim away the excess fabric. Only trim away the overcast edge at the top. Fold the fabric at the side and bottom edges 6 mm/¼ in to the wrong side, then fold the fabric again 13 mm/½ in to the wrong side. Baste, then sew the hem in place with small slipstitches. For the casing at the top edge, press the raw edge 6 mm/¼ in to the wrong side, then fold down 19 mm/¾ in; stitch in place with small slipstitches. Press gently. Insert a brass or wooden rod through the casing. (*see* p.118)

TABLE RUNNER

Cut a piece of evenweave fabric 2.5 cm/1 in larger all around than the desired finished size of your table runner. Overcast the raw edges. Decide where you wish to place the design. Embroider your chosen design, adding a border all around the table runner if desired. Carefully press the finished embroidery. Cut away excess fabric, leaving 19 mm/ ¾ in for hemming. Fold the

fabric 6 mm/¼ in to the wrong side, then fold the fabric again, this time 13 mm/½ in to the wrong side. Baste, then sew the hem in place with small slipstitches. Press gently. (*see* p.126)

CURTAIN TIEBACK or LAMPSHADE TRIM

Cut evenweave fabric slightly longer than required and wide enough for the design plus 13 mm/½ in. Overcast the raw edges. Embroider a border design along the centre of the fabric. Gently press the finished embroidery. Cut a matching piece of interfacing and lining. Baste the interfacing to the wrong side of the embroidery. With right sides facing, stitch the lining to the embroidery making a 13 mm/½ in seam. Turn right side out and press lightly. For the tieback, fold the raw edges inside and slipstitch in place. Apply Velcro to secure the ends together. For the lampshade trim, fold raw edges at one end to the wrong side. Slipstitch or glue the embroidery around the bottom edge of the lampshade, slipping the raw edges inside the folded edge. Slipstitch to secure. (*see* p.50)

CURTAIN

Measure your window and make a curtain using an evenweave fabric; the curtain should not be very full. Hem the bottom edge of the curtain, but not the sides. Overcast the raw edges. Begin working a border design in the

exact centre of the fabric, just above the hem. Work outward to each side edge. When finished, hem the side edges of the curtain. Gently press the finished embroidery. (*see* p.60)

CUSHION

Calculate the finished size of your design using the formula on page 6; cut evenweave fabric 2.5 cm/ 1 in larger than the calculated size all around. Overcast the raw edges. Work the design in the centre of the fabric. Carefully press the finished embroidery. Trim away the excess fabric leaving a 13 mm/½ in seam allowance all around. Cut a matching piece of fabric for the back. With right sides facing, stitch the back to the front making a 6 mm/¼ in seam and leaving an opening for turning. Turn to the right side and stuff with kapok or polyester fibrefill until plump. Fold the raw edges at the opening inside and slipstitch the opening closed. (*see* p.100)

BATH TOWEL EDGING

Cut evenweave fabric slightly longer than your towel and wide enough for the design plus 13 mm/½ in. Overcast the raw edges. Embroider a border design along the centre of the fabric. Gently press the finished embroidery. Trim off the overcast edges. Fold the raw edges of the embroidery 6 mm/¼ in to the wrong side and baste to your towel; slipstitch securely along each edge.

• FOR THE KITCHEN AND DINING ROOM •

POT HOLDER

Cut a piece of evenweave fabric about 18–23 cm/7–9 in square. Overcast the raw edges. Select a design that will fit nicely on the fabric and embroider the design in the centre. Gently press the finished embroidery. Trim off the overcast edges, then cut padding and a back to the same size; use two to three layers of cotton or wool padding; do not use polyester. Sandwich the padding between the embroidery and the back; baste the edges together. Use bias binding to finish the edges of the potholder, allowing excess binding at one corner to make a hanging loop. (*see* p.80)

SHELF BORDER

Cut evenweave fabric slightly longer than your shelf and wide enough for the design plus 13 mm/½ in. Overcast the raw edges. Embroider a border design along the centre of the fabric. Gently press the finished embroidery. Trim off the overcast edges. Cut a matching piece of interfacing. Baste the interfacing to the wrong side of the embroidery. Fold the raw edges of the embroidery 6 mm/¼ in to the wrong side and secure to the interfacing with small slipstitches. Press lightly. Thumbtack or glue the border to the front of your cupboard shelf. (*see* p.62)

PLACEMAT

Cut a piece of evenweave fabric 2.5 cm/1 in larger all around than the desired finished size of your placemat; a good finished size is about 35 × 45 cm/14 × 18 in. Overcast the raw edges. Decide where you wish to place the design – an attractive arrangement is to centre the design between the top and bottom edges along the left-hand edge of the fabric. Embroider your chosen design, adding a border all around the placemat if desired. Carefully press the finished embroidery. Cut away excess fabric, leaving 19 mm/ ¾ in for hemming. Fold the fabric 6 mm/¼ in to the wrong side, then fold the fabric again, this time 13 mm/½ in to the wrong side. Baste, then sew the hem in place with small slipstitches. Press gently. (*see* p.108)

ROUND TABLECLOTH or CENTREPIECE

Calculate the finished size of your design using the formula on page 6; cut evenweave fabric 3.8 cm/ 1½ in larger than the calculated size all around. Overcast the raw edges. Find the exact centre of the fabric and the design; mark fabric with a basting thread. Count from the centre of the graph and the fabric to start the design. Work the graph, which is one-quarter of the design, as shown.

Then turn the fabric clockwise and work the next quarter. Continue turning and repeating the quarter pattern twice more until the design is finished. Carefully press the finished embroidery. Measure 3 cm/1¼ in away from the outer edge of the embroidery and trim off the excess fabric. Fold the fabric 6 mm/¼ in to the wrong side twice. Baste, then sew the hem in place with small slipstitches. Press gently. (*see* p.75)

ROUND DOILY or TRAY CLOTH

Work as for the tablecloth except cut your evenweave fabric 2.5 cm/1 in larger than the calculated size of the project all around.

SIX-STRAND EMBROIDERY COTTON (FLOSS) CONVERSION CHART

Key:　　T = Possible substitute　　★ = Close match　　— = No match

DMC No.	Royal Mouliné No.	Bates/Anchor No.	DMC No.	Royal Mouliné No.	Bates/Anchor No.	DMC No.	Royal Mouliné No.	Bates/Anchor No.	DMC No.	Royal Mouliné No.	Bates/Anchor No.	DMC No.	Royal Mouliné No.	Bates/Anchor No.	DMC No.	Royal Mouliné No.	Bates/Anchor No.
White	1001	2	437	8200★	362	680	6260★	901	816	2530	44★	936	5260T	269	3326	2115★	25★
Ecru	8600	926	444	6155★	291	699	5375	923★	817	2415T	19	937	5260	268	3328	2045	11★
208	3335★	110★	445	6000	288	700	5365★	229	818	2505★	48	938	8430	381	3340	–	329
209	3415★	105	451	–	399★	701	5365★	227	819	2000	892★	939	4405	127	3341	–	328
210	3320★	104	452	–	399★	702	5330	239	820	4345	134	943	4935★	188★	3345	5025T	268★
211	3410	108★	453	1015T	397★	703	5320	238	822	8605★	387★	945	8020★	347★	3346	5220T	257★
221	2570	897★	469	5255	267★	704	5310★	256★	823	4400★	150	946	7230★	332★	3347	5210★	266★
223	2555	894	470	5255★	267	712	8600★	387★	824	4225	164★	947	7255★	330★	3348	5270★	265
224	2545	893	471	5245	266★	718	3015★	88	825	4215	162★	948	8070	778★	3350	2220	42★
225	2540	892	472	5240	264★	720	–	326	826	4210	161★	950	8020T	4146	3354	2210	74★
300	8330	352★	498	2425T	20★	721	–	324★	827	4605	159★	951	8020T	366★	3362	–	862★
301	8315★	349★	500	5125	879★	722	–	323★	828	4850	158★	954	5455★	203★	3363	–	861★
304	2415★	47★	501	5120★	878	725	6215	306★	829	5825	906	955	5450	206★	3364	–	843★
307	6005★	289★	502	5110	876	726	6150★	295	830	5825★	889★	956	2170★	40★	3371	8435	382
309	2525★	42★	503	5105	875	727	6135	293	831	5825T	889★	957	2160T	40★	3607	–	87★
310	1002	403	504	5100	213★	729	6255	890	832	5815	907	958	–	187	3608	–	86
311	4275T	149★	517	–	169★	730	–	924★	833	5815★	874★	959	–	186	3609	–	85
312	–	147★	518	4860★	168★	731	–	281★	834	5810★	874	961	2515★	76★	3685	2335	70★
315	3130	896★	519	4855T	167★	732	5925T	281★	838	8425★	380	962	2515	76★	3687	2325	69★
316	3120	895★	520	–	862★	733	–	280★	839	8560★	380★	963	2505	49★	3688	2320	66★
317	1030★	400★	522	–	859★	734	–	279★	840	8555★	379★	964	–	185	3689	2310	49
318	1020★	399★	523	–	859★	738	8245★	942	841	8550★	378★	966	5150★	214★	3705	–	35★
319	5025	246★	524	–	858★	739	8240★	885★	842	8505★	376★	970	7040	316★	3706	–	28★
320	5015	216★	535	1115T	401★	740	7045	316	844	1115T	401★	971	7045	316★	3708	–	26★
321	2415	47	543	8500	933★	741	6125	304	869	8720★	944★	972	6120★	298	48	9000★	1201★
322	–	978★	550	3380★	102★	742	6120	303	890	5025★	879★	973	6015	290	51	9014	1220
326	2530★	59★	552	3370★	101	743	6210	297	891	2135	35★	975	8365	355★	52	9006	1208
327	3365★	101★	553	3360	98	744	6110★	301★	892	2130	28	976	8355	308★	53	–	–
333	–	119	554	3355★	96★	745	6105	300★	893	2125★	27	977	8350	307★	57	9002	1203
334	4250T	145	561	–	212★	746	6100	386★	894	2115T	26	986	5430	246★	61	9013T	1218★
335	2525T	42★	562	–	210★	747	4850	158★	895	5430★	246★	987	5020T	244★	62	9000T	1201★
336	4270★	149★	563	–	208★	754	8075	778★	898	8425★	360	988	5295T	243★	67	–	1211★
340	–	118	564	–	203★	758	8080	868	899	2515	27★	989	5405T	242★	69	–	1218★
341	–	117	580	5935	267★	760	2035	9★	900	7230★	333	991	5165T	189★	75	9002	1206★
347	2425★	13★	581	5925	266★	761	2030	8★	902	–	72★	992	4925★	187★	90	9012★	1217
349	2400	13	597	4860★	168★	762	1010★	397★	904	5295★	258★	993	4915★	186★	91	9008★	1211
350	2045T	11	598	4855★	167★	772	–	264★	905	5295	258★	995	4710	410	92	9011T	1216★
351	2015T	11★	600	2225★	59★	775	4600★	128★	906	5285★	256★	996	4700	433	93	9007★	1210★
352	2015	10★	601	2225★	78★	776	2110★	24★	907	5280★	255	3011	5525T	845★	94	9011★	1216
353	2020★	8★	602	2640★	77★	778	3110	968★	909	5370	229★	3012	5525★	844★	95	9006T	1208★
355	8095	5968	603	2720★	76★	780	8215★	310★	910	5370★	228★	3013	5515	842★	99	9005T	1207★
356	8090	5975★	604	2710	75★	781	8215	309★	911	5465★	205★	3021	–	382★	101	9009★	1213★
367	5020	216★	605	2155	50★	782	6230	308	912	5465	205	3022	–	8581★	102	–	1208★
368	5005★	240★	606	7260	335	783	6220★	307	913	5460★	209	3023	–	8581★	103	–	1210★
369	5005	213★	608	7255	333★	791	4165★	941★	915	3030	89★	3024	1100	900★	104	9012	1217
370	–	889★	610	5825T	889★	792	4155T	940	917	3020★	89★	3031	–	905★	105	9013★	1218
371	–	888★	611	5735T	898	793	4155	121	918	8330★	341★	3032	8620T	903★	106	9002T	1203★
372	–	887★	612	8815★	832	794	4145	120★	919	8095★	341★	3033	8610★	388★	107	9003	1204
400	8325★	351	613	5605★	956★	796	4340	133★	920	8060★	339★	3041	3215★	871	108	9014★	1220★
402	8305★	347★	632	8530	936★	797	4265★	132★	921	8060T	349★	3042	3205★	869	111	–	1218★
407	8005	882★	640	8625	903	798	4255	131★	922	8315T	324★	3045	6260T	373★	112	9003T	1204★
413	1025★	401	642	8620★	392	799	4250★	130★	924	4830T	851★	3046	5810	887★	113	9007★	1210★
414	1020★	400★	644	8800	830	800	4310	128	926	4820★	779★	3047	5805	886★	114	9010	1215
415	1015	398	645	1115	905★	801	8405	357★	927	4810T	849★	3051	5530T	846★	115	9004	1206
420	8720★	375★	646	1115★	8581	806	4870T	169★	928	1010T	900★	3052	5060★	859★	121	9007	1210
422	8710★	373★	647	1110	8581★	807	4860★	168★	930	4510	922★	3053	5055★	859★	122	9010T	1215★
433	8265	371★	648	1100★	900	809	4145★	130★	931	4505	921★	3064	8005★	914★	123	–	1213★
434	8215	309	666	2405	46	813	4610★	160★	932	4500	920★	3072	4805★	397★	124	9007T	1210★
435	8210★	369★	676	6250	891	814	2340T	44★	934	5070T	862★	3078	6130	292★	125	9009	1213
436	8205	363★	677	–	886★	815	2530★	43	935	5225T	862★	3325	4200	159★	126	9006★	1208★

Small Motifs

Animals

• BIB WITH CAT AND BUTTERFLY •

Material: linen, 10 threads per cm.
Cutting size: 30 × 30 cm/12 × 12 in.
Finished size (motif): 10.5 × 7 cm/ 4¼ × 2¾ in.
Thread: DMC embroidery floss. Use 2 strands of floss in the needle.

Cat and butterfly

⊡	973	canary yellow
∧	741	medium yellow-orange
⊙	435	bright tan
⊠	414	medium gray
■	844	dark slate
–	844	dark slate (backstitch)

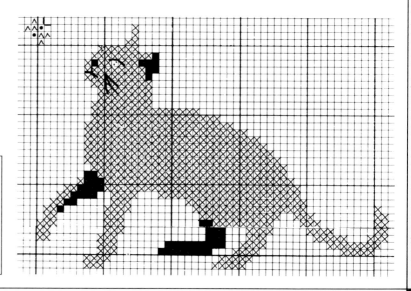

• TEDDY-BEAR •

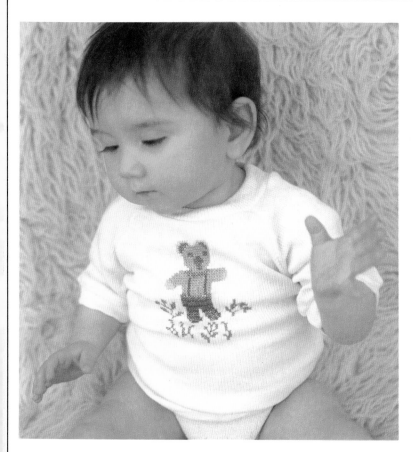

• TEDDY-BEAR •

Material: waste canvas on plain fabric.

Cutting size (canvas): 15 × 12 cm/ 6 × 4¾ in.

Finished size: 10 × 7.5 cm/4 × 3 in.

Thread: DMC embroidery floss. Use 2 strands of floss in the needle.

Teddy-bear		
⧄	783	dark gold
⊞	891	dark coral
∧	738	ice tan
L	518	bright cornflower blue
•	798	dark Dresden blue
⊠	906	medium emerald green
−		medium emerald green (backstitch)
◣	433	light chocolate brown

Work the cross-stitches on plain fabric using waste canvas; the motif's size will depend on the fineness of the canvas. The thread count on the canvas used here was 4½ stitches per cm/11 stitches per in. See page 8 for instructions on using waste canvas.

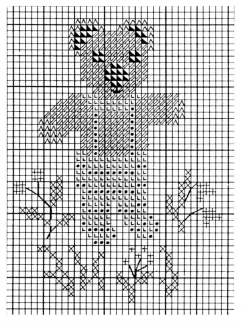

• WHITE HORSE •

Material: beige linen, 8 threads per cm.
Cutting size: 35 × 35 cm/13¾ × 13¾ in.
Finished size: 28 × 28 cm/11 × 11 in.
Thread: DMC embroidery floss. Use 3 strands of floss in the needle. Use 1 strand of pearl cotton no. 8 in the needle.

White horse		
◻		white pearl cotton no. 8
⊠	907	light emerald green
⊡	906	medium emerald green
◼	904	dark emerald green
◿	3024	pale gunmetal
◫	647	light slate
◣	645	bright slate
❘	645	bright slate (backstitch)

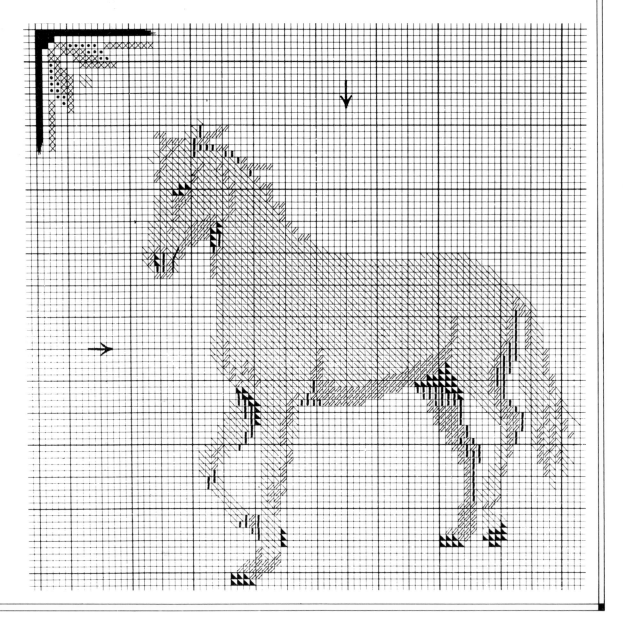

17

• POLAR BEAR •

Material: blue cotton Aida with 4½ stitches per cm/14 stitches per in.
Cutting size: 22 × 16 cm/8¾ × 6¼ in.
Finished size: 9 × 6 cm/3½ × 2¼ in.

Thread: DMC embroidery floss. Use 3 strands of floss in the needle. Use 1 strand of pearl cotton no. 8 in the needle.

Polar bear

L		white pearl cotton no. 8
⊠	3033	light sand
⧄	648	pale slate
■	310	black

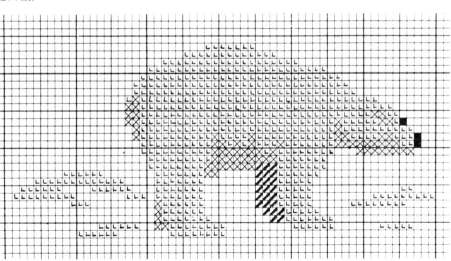

• Samples of Insects •

Material: linen, 8 threads per cm.
Thread: DMC embroidery floss. Use 3 strands of floss in the needle.
Cutting size: 25 × 25 cm/9¾ × 9¾ in.
Finished sizes:
Dragonfly: 7 × 7 cm/2¾ × 2¾ in.
Fly: 7 × 5 cm/2¾ × 2 in.
Ladybird: 3.5 × 3.5 cm/1½ × 1½ in.
Butterfly: 6 × 7 cm/2¼ × 2¾ in.

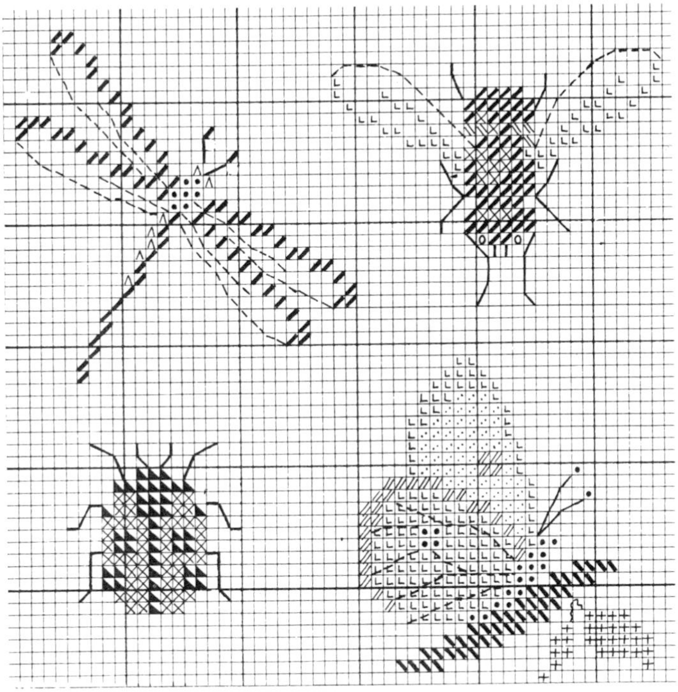

Dragonfly

- △ 783 dark gold
- ··· 644 light ash (backstitch)
- • 420 light acorn
- ⁄ 844 dark slate
- – 844 dark slate (backstitch)

Fly

- ○ 921 light rust
- ☒ 987 dark grass green
- ⧅ 611 medium camel
- ▨ 648 pale slate
- ··· 648 pale slate (backstitch)
- ⁄ 844 dark slate
- – 844 dark slate (backstitch)

Ladybird

- ☒ 349 red-orange
- ◣ 310 black
- – 310 black (backstitch)

Butterfly

- ⋅ 973 canary yellow
- L 725 medium gold
- ▨ 783 dark gold
- ··· 783 dark gold (backstitch)
- • 832 dark brass
- – 832 dark brass (backstitch)
- ⧅ 611 medium camel
- + 3346 dark spring green

• SAMPLES OF ANIMALS •

Material: linen, 8 threads per cm.
Thread: DMC embroidery floss.
Use 3 strands of floss in the
needle.
Cutting size: 25 × 25 cm/9¾ ×
9¾ in.
Finished sizes:
Kangaroo: 15.5 × 8 cm/6 ×
3¼ in.
Elephant: 7.5 × 7.5 cm/3 × 3 in.
Tortoise: 5.5 × 3.5 cm/2 ×
1½ in.

Kangaroo

☐	783	dark gold
☒	782	light coffee
■	838	dark brown

Elephant

☒	3047	light khaki brown
☐	647	light slate
☒	646	medium slate
◣	844	dark slate
—	844	dark slate (backstitch)

Tortoise

☒	647	light slate
☐	841	dusty brown
⊡	840	medium brown
■	839	deep brown
—	839	deep brown (backstitch)

Material: linen, 8 threads per cm.
Thread: DMC embroidery floss.
Use 3 strands of floss in the
needle.
Cutting size: 30 × 25 cm/12 ×
9¾ in.
Finished sizes:
Rooster: 7 × 7.5 cm/2¾ × 3 in.
Pig: 8.5 × 7 cm/3¼ × 2¾ in.
Mice (both): 6.5 × 5 cm/2½ ×
2 in.
Dolphin: 8.5 × 5.5 cm/3¼ × 2 in.

Rooster

⊙	783	dark gold
◣	817	cherry
⫽	904	dark emerald green
⊡	644	light ash
L	647	light slate
⊠	434	dark tan
▮	610	dark camel
◣	310	black

Pig

⊠	758	light salmon
◣	407	dark oatmeal
−	407	dark oatmeal (backstitch)

Mice

L	758	light salmon
⋀	646	medium slate
■	310	black

Dolphin

⊡		snow white
⋯	648	pale slate (backstitch)
◪	844	dark slate
◣	310	black

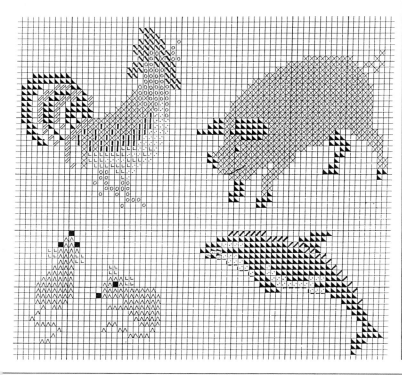

People

Material: beige linen, 8 threads per cm.
Cutting size: 40 × 50 cm/15¾ × 19¾ in.
Finished size: 34 × 44 cm/13¼ × 17¼ in.
Thread: DMC embroidery floss. Use 3 strands of floss in the needle.

Santa Claus

··		snow white
I	725	medium gold
⊟	950	oatmeal
⊘	781	medium coffee
◨	321	light ruby
⊠	606	dark orange-red
Ⅲ	797	royal blue
⋀	700	dark kelly green
⊡	632	sable brown
◣	310	black

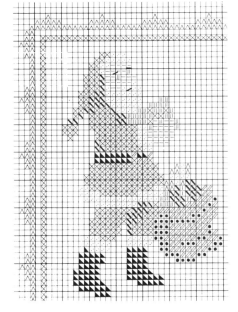

• SOCCER PLAYERS •

Material: light-green linen,
6 threads per cm.
Cutting size: 45 × 35 cm/
17¾ × 13¾ in.
Finished size: 32 × 22 cm/
12½ × 8¾ in.

Thread: DMC embroidery
floss. Use 6 strands of floss
in the needle.

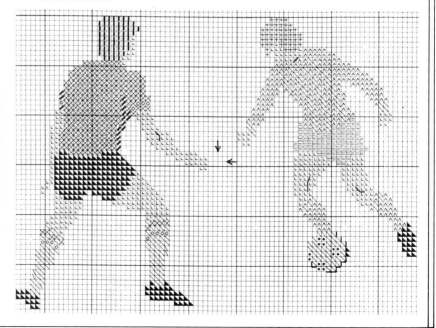

Soccer players

◣		snow white
L	758	light salmon
⊙	972	light orange
◮	349	red-orange
⊟	796	bright royal blue
⊠	699	deep kelly green
◿	895	dark hunter green
⊞	420	light acorn
▮	839	deep brown
–	839	deep brown
–		(backstitch)
⊡	844	dark slate
◤	310	black

• GOLF AND TENNIS PLAYERS •

Material: linen, 6 threads per cm.
Thread: DMC embroidery floss.
Use 6 strands of floss in the
needle.

Cuttting size: 30 × 35 cm/12 ×
13¾ in.
Finished sizes:
Golf: 7.5 × 15 cm/3 × 6 in.
Tennis: 13 × 16.5 cm/5 × 6½ in.

Golf player

◻		snow white
⌃	822	ash
L	758	light salmon
○	799	bright Dresden blue
▨	312	dark sky blue
■	336	medium navy blue
—	647	light slate (backstitch)
◣	801	medium chocolate brown
S	839	deep brown

Tennis player

◻		snow white
⌃	822	ash
L	758	light salmon
•	350	dark peach
▨	312	dark sky blue
—	647	light slate (backstitch)
◣	801	medium chocolate brown
~	801	medium chocolate brown (backstitch)

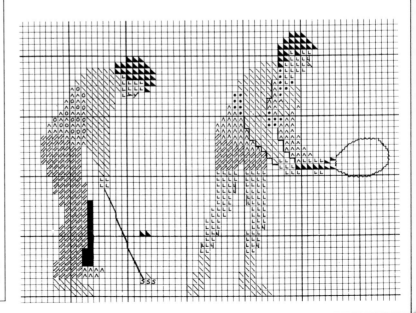

Birds

• PINCUSHION WITH BIRDS AND BERRIES •

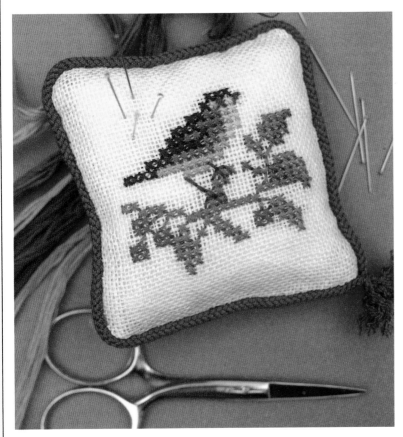

Material: linen, 8 threads per cm.
Cutting size: 2 pieces, 12 × 12 cm/
4¾ × 4¾ in.
Finished size: 9 × 9 cm/3½ ×
3½ in.
Thread: DMC embroidery floss.
Use 3 strands of floss in the
needle.

Bird and berries

⊡	444	dark yellow
●	349	red-orange
◪	931	medium soldier blue
◣	311	light navy blue
⊙	906	medium emerald green
⊠	905	bright emerald green
L	734	pale olive
‖	3012	medium khaki
…	3012	medium khaki (backstitch)
■	610	dark camel
–	610	dark camel (backstitch)

See page 8 for instructions on
making a pincushion.

• PLATE LINER WITH GREAT TIT •

Material: linen, 10 threads per cm.
Cutting size: 20 × 20 cm/7¾ × 7¾ in.
Finished size: 15.5 × 15.5 cm/ 6 × 6 in.
Thread: DMC embroidery floss. Use 2 strands of floss in the needle.

Great tit

⊡		snow white
◨	822	pale ash
☒	831	light bronze
⌶	307	medium yellow
⊟	930	dark soldier blue
◪	924	dark teal
⊙	734	pale olive
⊘	472	pale avocado
⊞	471	light avocado
⫴	470	medium avocado
◣	937	deep avocado
⊡	611	medium camel
△	414	medium gray
◤	310	black

• PLATE LINER WITH ROBIN •

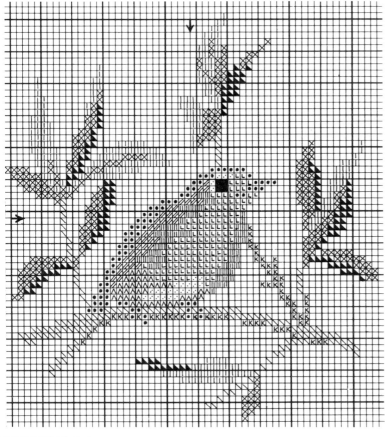

Material: 10 threads per cm.
Cutting size: 20 × 20 cm/7¾ ×
7¾ in.
Finished size: 15.5 × 15.5 cm/
6 × 6in.
Thread: DMC embroidery floss.
Use 2 strands of floss in the
needle.

Robin

⊡	822	pale ash
L	922	pale rust
⫲	921	light rust
⊡	471	light avocado
◢	937	deep avocado
☒	581	light apple green
⟍	3013	light khaki green
K	3012	medium khaki green
•	611	medium camel
△	3024	light stone
⧄	318	light gray
■	310	black

• Plate Liner with Greenfinch •

Material: linen, 10 threads per cm.
Cutting size: 20 × 20 cm/7¾ × 7¾ in.
Finished size: 15.5 × 15.5 cm/6 × 6 in.
Thread: DMC embroidery floss. Use 2 strands of floss in the needle.

Greenfinch

L	307	medium yellow
—	833	medium brass
o	921	light rust
■	919	medium rust
◺	472	pale avocado
Λ	471	light avocado
•	581	light apple green
X	3012	medium khaki green
–	3012	medium khaki green (backstitch)
‖	610	dark camel
◸	318	light gray
◣	317	dark gray

• PLATE LINER WITH BULLFINCH •

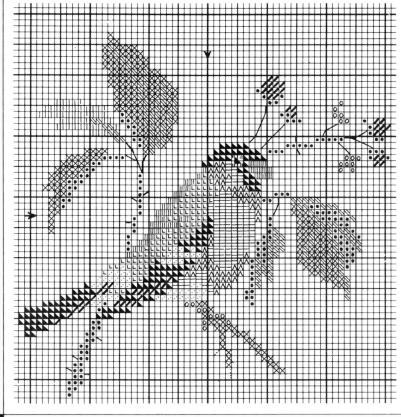

Material: linen, 10 threads per cm.
Cutting size: 20 × 20 cm/7¾ in × 7¾ in.
Finished size: 15.5 × 15.5 cm/ 6 × 6 in.
Thread: DMC embroidery floss. Use 2 strands of floss in the needle.

Bullfinch

⊡	822	pale ash
⊟	922	pale rust
⊿	921	light rust
⊡	471	light avocado
⊠	470	medium avocado
⋯	470	medium avocado (backstitch)
⧄	469	bright avocado
•	730	dark olive
—	730	dark olive (backstitch)
⊙	611	medium camel
L	318	light gray
‖	414	medium gray
⧄	844	dark slate
◥	310	black

• PLATE LINER WITH CHAFFINCH •

Material: linen, 10 threads per cm.

Cutting size: 20 × 20 cm/7¾ × 7¾ in.

Finished size: 15.5 × 15.5 cm/ 6 × 6 in.

Thread: DMC embroidery floss. Use 2 strands of floss in the needle.

Chaffinch

⊡		snow white
⊡	758	light salmon
⟑	3064	ginger
⊺	471	light avocado
⊠	581	light apple green
⊟	580	medium apple green
⫴	3012	medium khaki green
−	3012	medium khaki green (backstitch)
•	433	light chocolate brown
◨	3024	light stone
◪	414	medium gray
◣	844	dark slate

• BIB WITH BLUE TIT •

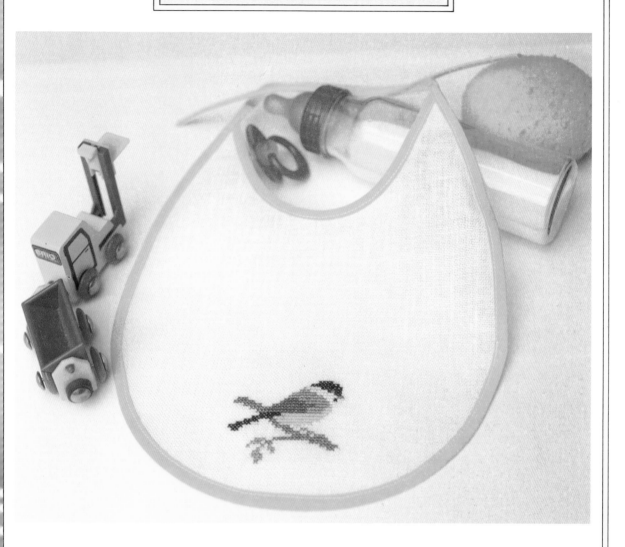

Material: linen, 10 threads
per cm.
Cutting size: 30 × 30 cm/12 ×
12 in.
Finished size (motif): 6 × 5 cm/
2¼ × 2 in.
Thread: DMC embroidery floss.
Use 2 strands of floss in the
needle.

See page 9 for instructions on
making a bib.

Blue tit

⊡		snow white
⌴	725	medium gold
⊡	825	deep blue
◣	823	dark navy blue
⟁	989	light grass green
⧄	611	medium camel
⊙	414	medium gray

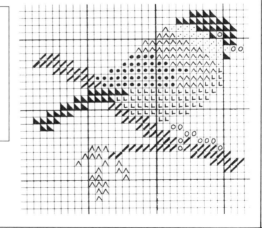

• FOUR SMALL MOTIFS •

Material: linen, 8 threads per cm.
Thread: DMC embroidery floss.
Use 3 strands of floss in the
needle.
Cutting size: 20 × 20 cm/7¾ ×
7¾ in.
Finished sizes:
Bird: 6 × 3.5 cm/2¼ × 1½ in.
Duck: 4 × 4 cm/1½ × 1½ in.
Bouquet: 4.5 × 5 cm/1¾ × 2 in.
Wreath: 5.5 × 3 cm/2 × 1¼ in.

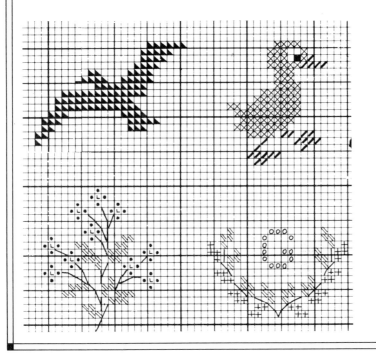

Flying bird

◣ 645   bright slate

Duck

⊠ 972   light orange
◪ 970   medium orange
■ 310   black

Bouquet

Ⓛ 743   dark lemon yellow
• 893   medium coral
◩ 988   medium grass green
— 988   medium grass green
         (backstitch)

Wreath

⊙ 208   dark lavender
— 581   light apple green
         (backstitch)
⊞ 471   light avocado
◩ 988   medium grass green

Flowers

• BREADMAT WITH FLORAL WREATH •

Material: linen, 10 threads per cm.

Cutting size: 30 × 30 cm/12 × 12 in.

Finished size: 27 × 27 cm/10¾ × 10¾ in.

Thread: DMC embroidery floss. Use 2 strands of floss in the needle.

Floral wreath

⊡	444	dark yellow
⧅	3326	dark pink
⊙	961	dark strawberry
L	209	deep lavender
▮	793	medium marine blue
⊠	906	medium emerald green
–	906	medium emerald green (backstitch)

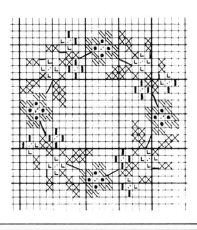

• MATCHBOX WITH EMBROIDERED HAREBELL •

Material: linen with 10 threads per cm.
Cutting size: 15 × 10 cm/6 × 4 in.
Finished size: 12.5 × 7 cm/5 × 2¾ in.
Thread: DMC embroidery floss. Use 2 strands of floss in the needle.

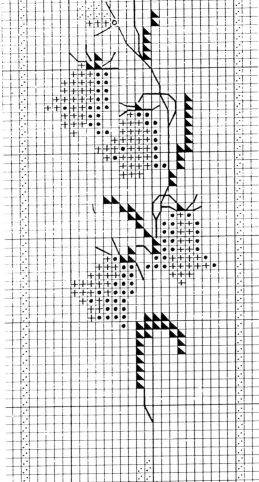

Harebell

- ⊡ 211 light lavender
- ⊞ 794 light marine blue
- ● 793 medium marine blue
- ⊙ 3347 medium spring green
- − 3347 medium spring green (backstitch)
- ◣ 3346 dark spring green

See page 9 for instructions on making a matchbox cover.

• MATCHBOX WITH EMBROIDERED • CORNFLOWER

Material: linen, 10 threads per cm.
Cutting size: 15 × 10 cm/6 × 4 in.
Finished size: 12.5 × 7cm/5 × 2¾ in.
Thread: DMC embroidery floss. Use 2 strands of floss in the needle.

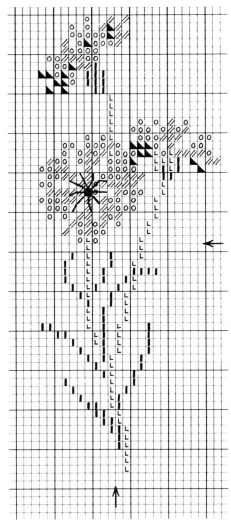

Cornflower

■	552	bright lilac
–	552	bright lilac (backstitch)
⊡	794	light marine blue
▨	793	medium marine blue
◣	792	bright marine blue
Ⓛ	3053	light sage
Ⅱ	3052	medium sage

See page 9 for instructions on making a matchbox cover.

● *SMALL BOUQUET TO SEW ON COLLAR* ●
OR *HANDKERCHIEF*

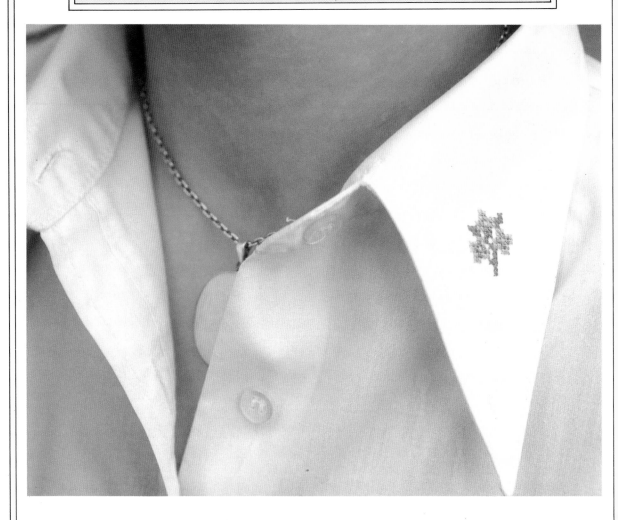

Material: waste canvas on plain fabric.
Cutting size (canvas): 6 × 6 cm/ 2¼ × 2¼ in.
Finished size (motif): 2 × 2cm/ ¾ × ¾ in.
Thread: DMC embroidery floss. Use 2 strands of floss in the needle.

Small bouquet

●	725	medium gold
⊡	813	medium blue
◪	793	medium marine blue
⊠	906	medium emerald green

Work the cross-stitches on plain fabric using waste canvas; the bouquet's size will depend on the fineness of the canvas. The thread count on the canvas used here was 6 stitches per cm/15 stitches per in. See page 8 for instructions on using waste canvas.

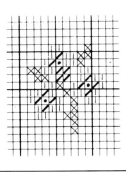

• PINCUSHION WITH GENTIAN •

Material: linen, 10 threads
per cm.
Cutting size: 16 × 16 cm/6¼ ×
6¼ in.
Finished size: 7 × 7 cm/2¾ ×
2¾ in.
Thread: DMC embroidery floss.
Use 2 strands of floss in the
needle.

See page 11 for instructions on
working a round design;

Gentian

⬚ ·	906	snow white
⊤	932	light soldier blue
∧	799	bright Dresden blue
▨	798	dark Dresden blue
■	797	royal blue
L	471	light avocado
⊡ •	988	medium grass green

see page 8 for instructions on
making a pincushion.

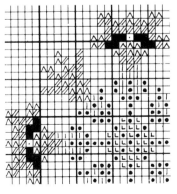

• SIX SMALL MOTIFS •

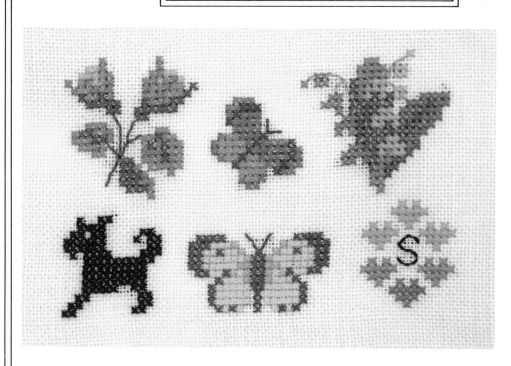

Material: linen, 8 threads per cm.
Thread: DMC embroidery floss.
Use 3 strands of floss in the
needle.
Cutting size: 25 × 18cm/9¾ ×
7 in.
Finished sizes:
Roses: 5 × 5 cm/2 × 2 in.
Brown butterfly: 3.5 × 3.5 cm/
1½ × 1½ in.
Blue flowers: 5.5 × 5 cm/2 ×
2 in.

Dog: 3.75 × 3.5 cm/1½ × 1½ in.
Yellow butterfly: 5.5 × 2.75 cm/
2 × 1¼ in.
Hearts: 3.5 × 4 cm/1½ × 1½ in.

Roses
Ⓛ	3326	dark pink
⊡	891	dark coral
⊠	989	light grass green
⧄	904	dark emerald green
−	904	dark emerald green (backstitch)

Brown butterfly
⊞	921	light rust
⧅	434	dark tan
◣	610	dark camel
−	610	dark camel (backstitch)

Blue flowers
⊟	794	light marine blue
△	793	medium marine blue
−	471	light avocado (backstitch)
⊠	989	light grass green
⧄	904	dark emerald green

Dog
◳	310	black

Yellow butterfly
⊤	444	dark yellow
⧄	783	dark gold
◣	610	dark camel
−	610	dark camel (backstitch)

Hearts
⊡	893	medium coral
◳	891	dark coral
⊟	321	light ruby
−	310	black

• BIB WITH FLORAL SWAG •

Materials: cotton Aida, 5½ stitches per cm.
Cutting size: 25 × 30 cm/9¾ × 12 in.
Finished size (motif): 10 × 6 cm/ 4 × 2¼ in.
Thread: DMC embroidery floss. Use 2 strands of floss in the needle.

See page 9 for instructions on making a bib.

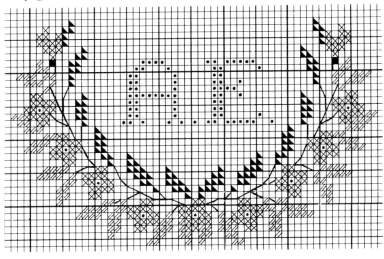

Floral swag

⊡	444	dark yellow
–	831	light bronze (backstitch)
⊠	48	variegated rose
⊘	907	light emerald green
◣	906	medium emerald green
■	831	light bronze

• JAR COVERS •

Material: linen, 10 threads per cm.
Cutting size: to cover diameter of jar lid plus 6 cm/2½ in.
Finished sizes: diameters plus 6 cm/2½ in. The design shown is 13 × 13 cm/5 × 5 in.

Thread: DMC embroidery floss. Use 2 strands of floss in the needle.

Redcurrant

⊡	758	light salmon
▨	349	red-orange
◣	832	dark brass
–	471	light avocado (backstitch)
⊡	905	bright emerald green
■	3021	dark gunmetal

Strawberry

⊡	905	green
–	905	green (backstitch)
◣	832	golden
▨	349	dark red
L	351	medium red
⊡	758	light red

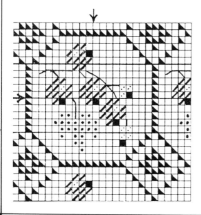

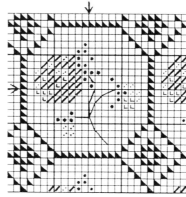

• *LAVENDER BAGS* •

Material: linen, 8 threads per cm.
Thread: DMC embroidery floss.
Use 3 strands of floss in the
needle.
Cutting size: 2 pieces, 11 × 15
cm/4¼ × 6 in. Embroider one
fabric only.

Finished sizes:
Floral wreath: 5.5 × 5.5 cm/2 ×
2 in.
Flowers: 5 × 6 cm/2 × 2¼ in.

Wreath		
⊡	725	medium gold
△	793	medium marine blue
●	798	dark Dresden blue
⊠	906	medium emerald green
◣	831	light bronze
—	831	light bronze (backstitch)

Flowers		
⊙	725	medium gold
L	3326	dark pink
◥	961	dark strawberry
◣	553	medium lilac
⊠	906	medium emerald green
—	831	light bronze (backstitch)

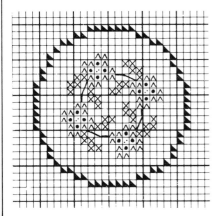

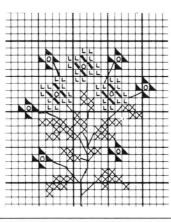

• SMALL BOUQUET •

Material: waste canvas on plain fabric.
Cutting size (canvas): 10 × 9 cm/4 × 3½ in.

Finished size (motif): 6.5 × 5 cm/ 2½ × 2 in.
Thread: DMC embroidery floss. Use 2 strands of floss in the needle.

Work the cross-stitches on plain fabric using waste canvas; the bouquet's size will depend on the fineness of the canvas. The thread count on the canvas used here was 4½ stitches per cm/11 stitches per inch. See page 8 for instructions on using waste canvas.

Small bouquet

•	743	dark lemon yellow
▨	3326	dark pink
◣	961	dark strawberry
⊠	93	variegated blue
⬕	989	light grass green
–	989	light grass green (backstitch)

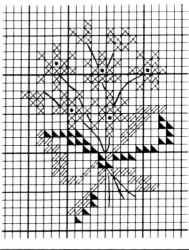

• PLACEMAT WITH CHRISTMAS TREE •

Material: linen, 8 threads per cm.
Cutting size: 40 × 50 cm/15¾ × 19¾ in.
Finished size: 34 × 44 cm/13¼ × 17¼ in.
Thread: DMC embroidery floss. Use 3 strands of floss in the needle.

Christmas tree

L	725	medium gold
~	725	medium golden (backstitch)
×	321	light ruby
⊘	799	bright Dresden blue
◣	311	light navy blue
•	700	dark kelly green
⊓	311	light navy blue

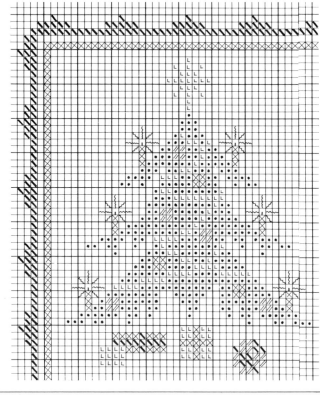

• SPECTACLE CASE WITH FLOWERING TREE •

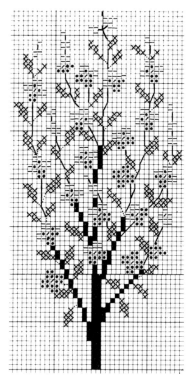

Material: linen, 10 threads per cm.

Cutting size: 2.5 cm/1 in larger than length and width measurement of spectacles.

Backing material: same size as linen.

Interfacing: 2 pieces same size as linen.

Thread: DMC embroidery floss. Use 2 strands of floss in the needle.

Flowering tree

⊟	3326	dark pink
⊡	335	medium carnation pink
⊘	972	light orange
⊠	906	medium emerald green
⋯	906	medium emerald green (backstitch)
■	830	medium bronze
–	830	medium bronze (backstitch)

Press the finished embroidery and the backing material. Iron-on or baste the interfacing to the wrong side of the embroidery and backing material. With right sides facing, stitch the embroidered linen to the backing material along the sides and bottom of the design, making a 1.2 cm/½ in seam. Trim away 6 mm/¼ in from the seam allowance; overcast the raw edges together. Fold the raw top edges 6 mm/¼ in to the inside twice; slipstitch in place.

Miscellaneous

• MUSHROOMS •

Material: cotton Aida, 5 stitches per cm.
Cutting size: 12 × 13 cm/4¾ × 5 in.
Finished size: 6 × 6.5 cm/2¼ × 2½ in.
Thread: DMC embroidery floss.

Use 2 strands of floss in the needle.

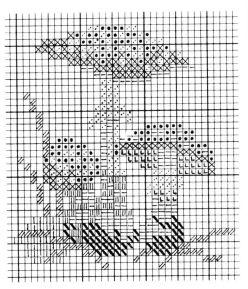

Mushrooms

☒	971	dark orange
•	900	dark pumpkin
▨	581	light apple green
Ⅱ	734	pale olive
⋅	822	pale ash
⊟	3033	light sand
Ⅱ	612	light camel
◣	840	medium brown
L	648	pale slate

• SAILING BOAT ON TIE •

Material: waste canvas on plain fabric.

Cutting size: 6 × 5 cm/2¼ × 2 in.

Finished size (motif): 2.75 × 2.5 cm/1¼ × 1 in.

Thread: DMC embroidery floss. Use 2 strands of floss in the needle.

Work the cross-stitches on plain fabric using waste canvas; the boat's size will depend on the fineness of the canvas. The thread count on the canvas used here was 6 stitches per cm/15 stitches per inch. See page 8 for instructions on using waste canvas.

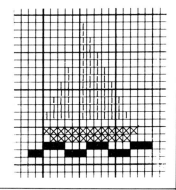

Sailing boat

⊡		snow white
⊠	309	bright carnation pink
■	797	royal blue

• PLACECARD – MOTIFS •

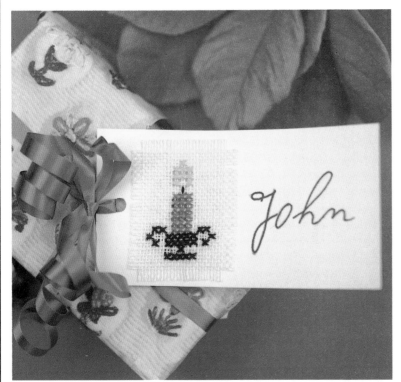

Material: linen, 10 threads per cm.
Cutting size: 3.5 × 4 cm/1½ × 1½ in.
Finished size: 2 × 3 cm/1 × 1¼ in.
Thread: DMC embroidery floss. Use 2 strands of floss in the needle.

Candle

⊙	972	light orange
⊠	606	dark orange-red
◣	310	black
–	310	black (backstitch)

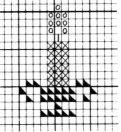

Material: linen, 10 threads per cm.
Cutting size: 3.75 × 3.5 cm/1½ × 1½ in.
Finished size: 2.5 × 3 cm/1 × 1¼ in.
Thread: DMC embroidery floss. Use 2 strands of floss in the needle.

Hanging heart

L	972	light orange
⊠	606	dark orange-red
◣	702	medium kelly green

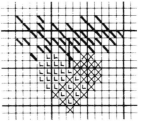

See instructions on page 8 for making placecards.

• CHRISTMAS CARD MOTIFS •

Material: linen, 10 threads per cm.
Cutting sizes:
Angel: 6 × 4 cm/2¼ × 1½ in.
Bird: 5 × 5 cm/2 × 2 in.

Finished sizes:
Angel: 5 × 3 cm/2 × 1¼ in.
Bird: 4 × 4 cm/1½ × 1½in.
Thread: DMC embroidery floss. Use 2 strands of floss in the needle.

Christmas angel

⊡	972	light orange
⟋	606	dark orange-red
⊓	813	medium blue
⧅	798	dark Dresden blue
⬚	950	oatmeal
⧄	781	medium coffee
–	813	medium blue (backstitch)

Bird with candle

⋯	972	light orange (backstitch)
⊠	606	dark orange-red
⊓	813	medium blue
⧄	798	dark Dresden blue
◼	311	light navy blue
◣	905	bright emerald green

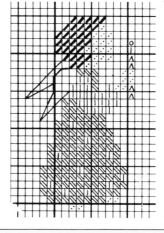

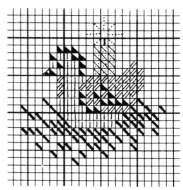

·3·

Border Designs

• BORDER FOR LAMPSHADE •

Material: white cotton Aida, 4½ stitches per cm.

Cutting size: 8 cm/3¼ in × size of lampshade.

Finished size: 3.75 cm/1½ in deep.

Thread: DMC embroidery floss. Use 2 strands of floss in the needle.

Geometric design

⊙	783	dark gold
–	783	dark gold (backstitch)
◣	920	bright rust
•	932	light soldier blue
⊠	470	medium avocado

See page 10 for instructions on making lampshade trim.

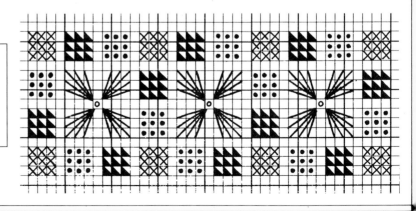

• CLASSICAL BORDER •

Material: linen, 8 threads per cm.
Cutting size: 15 cm/6 in deep.
Finished size: 7 cm/3¾ in deep.
Thread: DMC embroidery floss.
Use 3 strands of floss in the
needle.

Classical border

⊡	742	light yellow–orange
L	793	medium marine blue
●	792	bright marine blue
⊠	989	light grass green
◣	730	dark olive

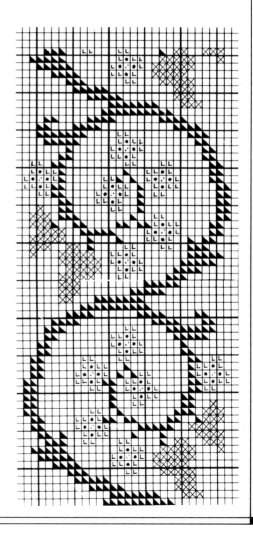

• SHELF BORDER WITH DUTCH TILES •

Material: linen, 10 threads
per cm.
Cutting size: 12 cm/4¾ in deep
and as long as your shelf.
Finished size: 8 cm/3¼ in deep.
Thread: DMC embroidery floss.
Use 2 strands of floss in the
needle.

Dutch tiles border

⊡	809	bright Dresden blue
⋯	809	bright Dresden blue (backstitch)
◥	797	royal blue
—	797	royal blue (backstitch)

See page 11 for instructions on
making a shelf border.

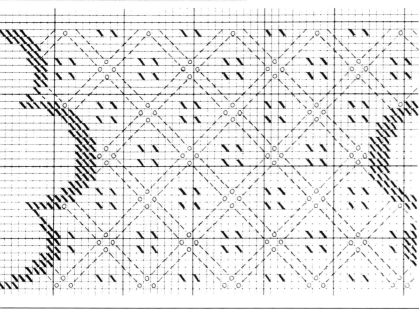

• SHELF BORDER •

Material: linen, 10 threads
per cm.
Cutting size: 11 cm/4¼ in deep
and as long as your shelf.
Finished size: 4.5 cm/1¾ in deep.
Thread: DMC embroidery floss.
Use 2 strands of floss in the
needle.

Floral border

⊡	972	light orange
▨	832	dark brass
⊺	813	medium blue
⊠	334	medium sky blue
⊡	798	dark Dresden blue
◣	433	light chocolate brown

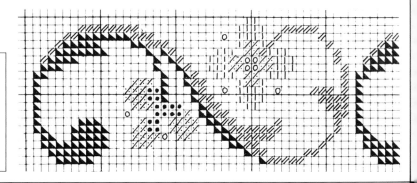

• CURTAIN WITH FOLK ART BORDER •

Material: beige cotton Aida, 4½ stitches per cm.
Cutting size: 50 cm/19¾ in and as long as required.
Finished size: 40 cm/15¾ in deep.
Thread: DMC embroidery floss. Use 3 strands of floss in the needle.

Folk art border

⊺	353	light peach
⧄	900	dark pumpkin
⊠	783	dark gold
•	731	bright olive
◣	801	medium chocolate brown

If you wish to sew on a white background instead of beige, use 972 light orange and 581 light apple green instead of 783 dark gold and 731 bright olive. See page 10 for instructions on making a curtain.

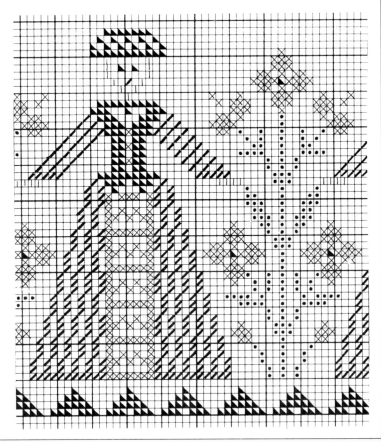

• SHELF BORDER WITH CHRISTMAS MOTIF •

Material: cotton Aida, 4½ stitches per cm.
Cutting size: 13 cm/5 in deep and as long as your shelf.
Finished size: 5.5 cm/2 in deep.
Thread: DMC embroidery floss. Use 3 strands of floss in the needle.

Hearts and pine border

L	725	medium gold
•	606	dark orange red
⊠	905	bright emerald green
■	831	light bronze

See page 11 for instructions on making a shelf border.

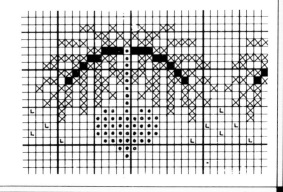

• SHELF BORDER WITH SCILLA •

Material: linen, 8 threads per cm.
Cutting size: 10 cm/4 in deep and
as long as your shelf.
Finished size: 6.5 cm/2½ in deep.
Thread: DMC embroidery floss.
Use 3 strands of floss in the
needle.

Scilla border

L	813	medium blue
∧	826	bright blue
•	825	deep blue
‖	3347	medium spring green
◥	988	medium grass green
✕	3012	medium khaki green
~	3012	medium khaki green (backstitch)

See page 11 for instructions on
making a shelf border.

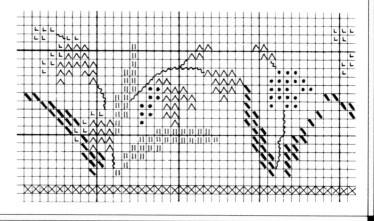

• CURTAIN WITH ROSES BORDER •

Material: linen, 8 threads per cm.
Cutting size: 45 cm/17¾ in deep
and as long as required.
Finished size: 38 cm/15 in deep.
Thread: DMC embroidery floss.
Use 3 strands of floss in the
needle.

Roses border

⊡	353	light peach
◨	352	medium peach
⊞	351	bright peach
▨	891	dark coral
•	326	dark carnation pink
L	471	light avocado
⊠	3347	medium spring green
▮	3346	dark spring green
∧	3012	medium khaki green
◣	830	medium bronze

See page 10 for instructions on
making a curtain.

• PHEASANT BORDER •

Material: white cotton Aida, 4½ stitches per cm.

Cutting size: 22 cm/8¾ in deep and as long as required.

Finished size: 14.5 cm/5¾ in deep.

Thread: DMC embroidery floss. Use 3 strands of floss in the needle.

Pheasant border

⊥	972	light orange
⊡	581	light apple green
⋀	435	bright tan
◢	433	light chocolate brown

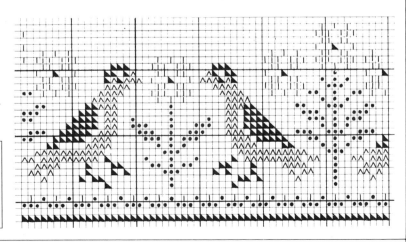

• CURTAIN WITH CHERRIES BORDER •

Material: linen, 8 threads per cm.
Cutting size: 40 cm/15¾ in and as
long as required.
Finished size: 35 cm/13¾ in deep.
Thread: DMC embroidery floss.
Use 3 strands of floss in the needle.

See page 10 for instructions on
making a curtain.

Cherries border		
⊡	353	light peach
⊞	350	dark peach
◪	817	cherry
■	816	claret
⊓	471	light avocado
◨	3347	medium spring green
⊟	3346	dark spring green
⊠	581	light apple green
⊡	580	medium apple green
▨	832	dark brass
⫼	840	medium brown
◣	838	dark brown

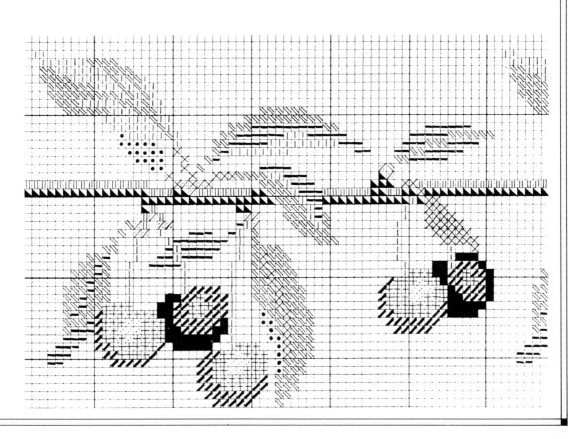

• SHELF BORDER WITH BLACKBIRDS •

Material: linen, 5 threads per cm.
Cutting size: 15 cm/6 in and as
long as required.
Finished size: 5.75 cm/2¼ in
deep.
Thread: DMC embroidery floss.
Use 3 strands of floss in the
needle.

Blackbird border

⊡	608	orange-red
△	907	light emerald green
▨	906	medium emerald green
⊞	611	medium camel
~	611	medium camel (backstitch)
◣	310	black
–	310	black (backstitch)

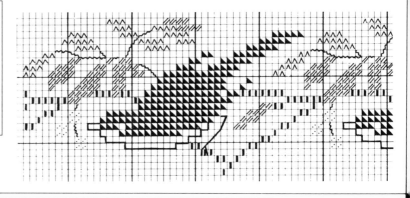

See page 11 for instructions on
making a shelf border.

• BORDER FOR LAMPSHADE WITH •
GREAT TIT ON FORSYTHIA

Material: linen, 10 threads per cm.

Cutting size: 13 cm/5 in × circumference of lampshade.

Thread: DMC embroidery floss. Use 2 strands of floss in the needle.

Great tit on forsythia border

⋅		ecru		⊞	471	light avocado
L	726	light gold		⊟	734	pale olive
⊙	725	medium gold		◩	733	light olive
△	931	medium soldier blue		–	733	light olive (backstitch)
⊡	823	dark navy blue		⊠	611	medium camel

See page 10 for instructions on making lampshade trim.

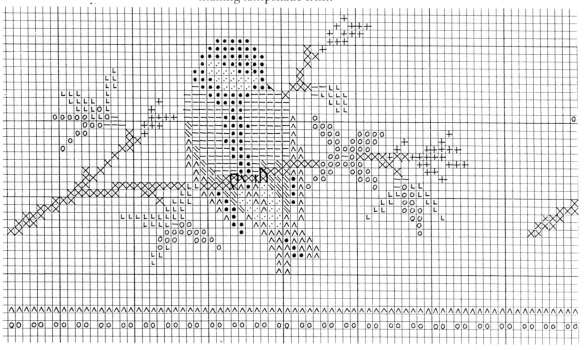

• PLACEMAT AND PLATE LINER •
WITH 'OLD AMERICA' (c.1800) BORDER

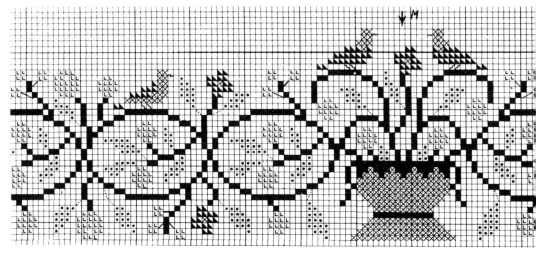

Placemat

Material: beige cotton Aida, 4½ stitches per cm.
Cutting size: 52 × 40 cm/20¾ × 15¾ in.
Finished size: 48 × 36 cm/19 × 14¼ in.
Thread: DMC embroidery floss. Use 3 strands of floss in the needle.

Begin embroidering the border design midway across the material and about 4 cm/1½ in up from bottom edge, starting with the midpoint of the design (see arrow).

Plate liner

Cutting size: 20 × 20 cm/8 in × 8 in.
Finished size: 15 × 15 cm/6 in × 6 in.

Early American design

⊡	606	dark orange-red
◣	815	burgundy
⊡	986	deep grass green
⊠	976	medium raisin
■	975	dark raisin
~	976	medium raisin (backstitch)
–	975	dark raisin (backstitch)
⋯	986	deep grass green (backstitch)

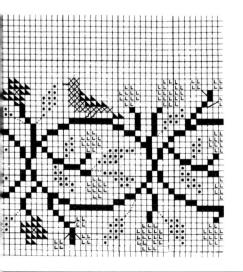

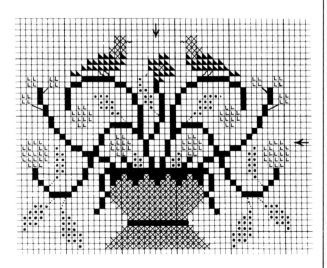

• BORDER WITH BIRDS •

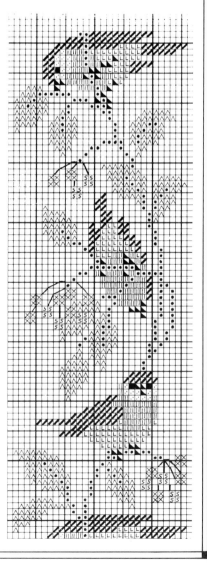

Material: cotton Aida, 4½ stitches
per cm.
Cutting size: 15 cm/6 in deep.
Finished size: 6.5 cm/2½ in wide.
Thread: DMC embroidery floss.
Use 3 strands of floss in the
needle.

Border with birds

⊡		snow white
L	725	medium gold
‖	783	dark gold
☒	350	dark peach
S	817	cherry
◪	336	medium navy blue
⋀	471	light avocado
⊡	3012	medium khaki green
−	3012	medium khaki green
		(backstitch)
◢	610	dark camel
■	310	black

• PLACEMAT WITH BUTTERFLY BORDER •

Material: beige linen, 8 threads per cm.
Cutting size: 44 × 38 cm/17¼ × 15 in.
Finished size: 44 × 34 cm/17¼ × 13¼ in.

Thread: DMC embroidery floss. Use 3 strands of floss in the needle.

Butterfly border

⊡		snow white
Ⓣ	712	ivory
Ⓛ	519	medium blue
⊡	518	bright cornflower blue
⋯	518	bright cornflower blue (backstitch)
⊙	783	dark gold
⋀	907	light emerald green
◪	905	bright emerald green
~	732	medium olive (backstitch)
◣	645	bright slate
–	645	bright slate (backstitch)

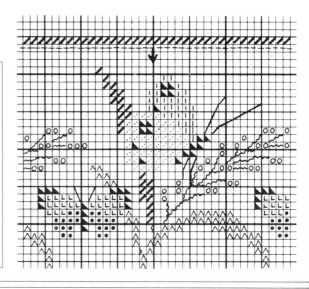

• PLACEMAT WITH DOGS BORDER •

Material: beige linen, 8 threads per cm.
Cutting size: 41 × 38 cm/16¼ × 15 in.
Finished size: 41 × 34 cm/16¼ × 13¼ in.

Thread: DMC embroidery floss. Use 3 strands of floss in the needle.

Border with dogs

⊡		snow white
⊠	946	medium pumpkin
⋯	946	medium pumpkin (backstitch)
△	907	light emerald green
◿	905	bright emerald green
⏐	3024	pale gunmetal
●	645	bright slate
−	645	bright slate (backstitch)
⫼	433	light chocolate brown
◣	310	black

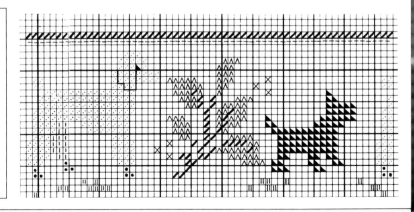

Round Designs

• HOLIDAY WREATH •

Material: linen, 8 threads per cm.
Cutting size: 45 × 45 cm/17¾ ×
17¾ in.
Finished size: 42 × 42 cm/16½ ×
16½ in.
Thread: DMC embroidery floss.
Use 3 strands of floss in the
needle. If using gold metallic
thread, use only 1 strand in the
needle.

Holiday wreath

⊡	725	medium (or metallic) gold
~	725	medium (or metallic) gold (backstitch)
▣	608	orange-red
L	927	light teal
⊠	502	medium lichen green (2)
◣	501	bright lichen green
■	420	light acorn brown
—	420	light acorn brown (backstitch)

See page 11 for instructions on
completing a round centrepiece.

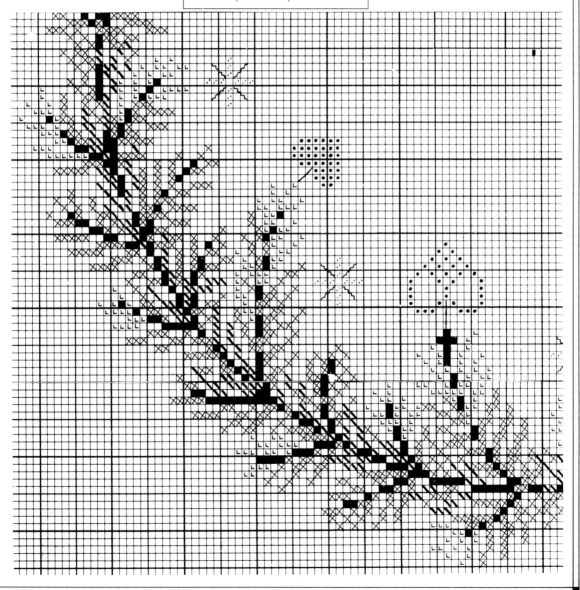

• CENTREPIECE WITH CIRCLE OF POPPIES •

Material: linen, 10 threads per cm.

Cutting size: 46 × 46 cm/18 × 18 in.

Finished size: 40 × 40 cm/15¾ × 15¾ in.

Thread: DMC embroidery floss. Use 2 strands of floss in the needle over 2 threads of fabric.

Circle of poppies

☒	352	medium peach
◩	351	bright peach
⫴	350	dark peach
Ⓒ	833	medium brass
−	833	medium brass (backstitch)
⊡	831	light bronze
⊟	471	light avocado
⟋	470	medium avocado
◪	3346	dark spring green
■	844	dark slate

See page 11 for instructions on completing a round centrepiece.

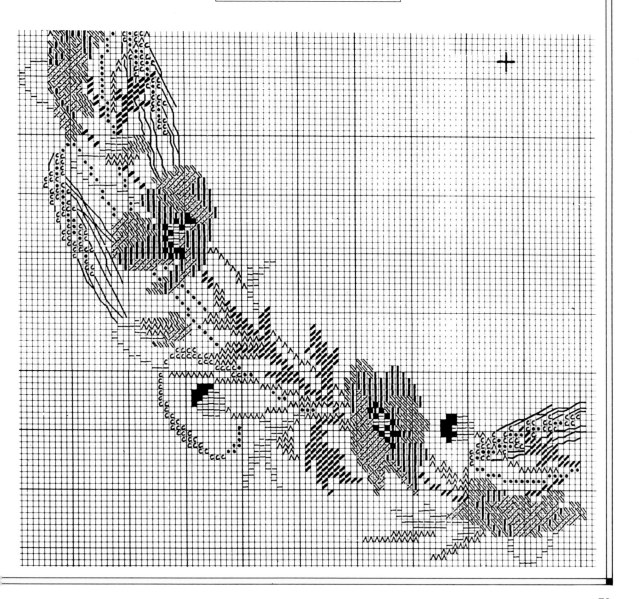

• PLATE LINER WITH CHRISTMAS MOTIF •

Material: cotton Aida, 4½ stitches per cm.

Cutting size: 17 × 17 cm/6¾ × 6¾ in.

Finished size: 13 × 13 cm/5 × 5 in.

Thread: DMC embroidery floss. Use 3 strands of floss in the needle. If using gold metallic thread, use only 1 strand in the needle.

Hearts and pine

L	725	medium (or metallic) gold
−	725	medium (or metallic) gold (backstitch)
•	606	dark orange-red
■	831	light bronze
✕	905	bright emerald green

See page 11 for instructions on completing a round doily.

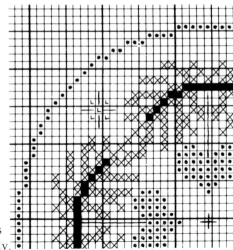

• ROUND TABLECLOTH WITH CROCUSES •

Instructions overleaf

ROUND TABLECLOTH WITH CROCUSES

Material: linen, 10 threads per cm.
Cutting size: 50 × 50 cm/19¾ × 19¾ in.
Finished size: approx. 44 cm/ 17¼ in in diameter.
Thread: DMC embroidery floss. Use 2 strands of floss in the needle.

Circle of crocuses

Symbol	No.	Colour
○	741	medium yellow orange
·	211	light lavender
⁄	554	light lilac
×	553	medium lilac
◖	552	bright lilac
⁚	3348	light spring green
V	320	medium moss green
↙	986	deep grass green
•	937	deep avocado

See page 11 for instructions on completing a round tablecloth.

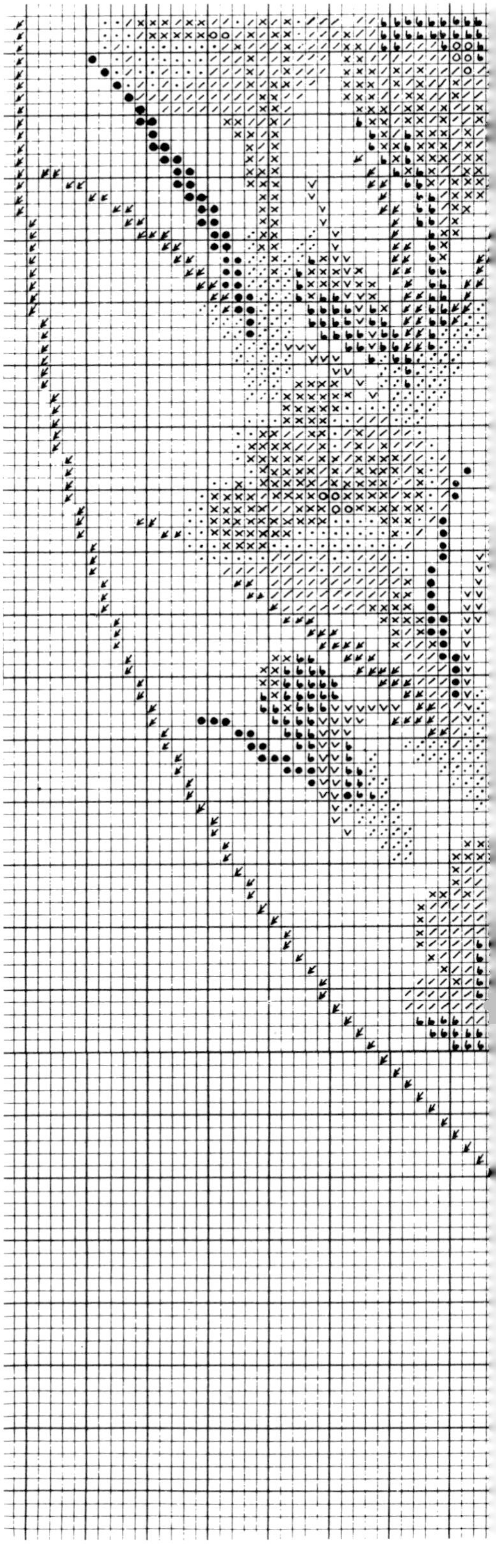

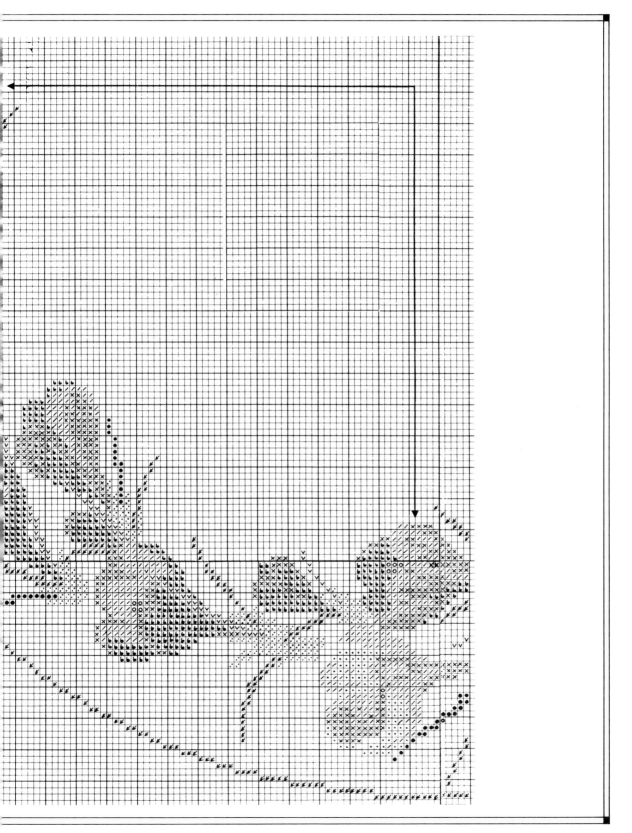

• CHAIR PILLOW WITH •
FLOWER BASKET IN A WREATH

Material: linen or burlap, 6 threads per cm.
Cutting size: 45 × 45 cm/17¾ × 17¾ in.
Finished size: 40 × 40 cm/15¾ × 15¾.
Thread: DMC embroidery floss. Use 3 strands of floss in the needle.

Flower basket in a wreath

L	3688	light dusty rose
✕	3687	medium dusty rose
I	3685	dark dusty rose
∧	471	light avocado
◿	470	medium avocado
◣	937	deep avocado
•	680	dark mustard
■	632	sable brown

• POT HOLDERS WITH DUCK AND ROOSTER •

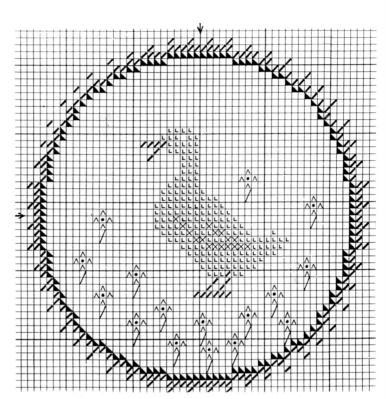

Material: Aida, 4½ stitches per cm.
Cutting size: 20 × 20 cm/7¾ × 7¾ in.
Finished size: 17 × 17 cm/6¾ × 6¾ in.
Thread: DMC embroidery floss. Use 3 strands of floss in the needle.

Duck

L		snow white
∧	307	medium yellow
◪	742	light yellow orange
◣	740	dark yellow orange
⊡	907	light emerald green
−	907	light emerald green (backstitch)
⊠	504	pale lichen green

Rooster

L		snow white
◪	742	light yellow orange
◣	740	dark yellow orange
S	606	dark orange-red
⊠	504	pale lichen green
⊡	907	light emerald green
■	911	medium malachite
--	740	dark yellow orange

Work the following additional backstitches: snow-white eye, deep-brown eyelashes and brows, and red-orange lips. See page 11 for instructions on making a pot holder.

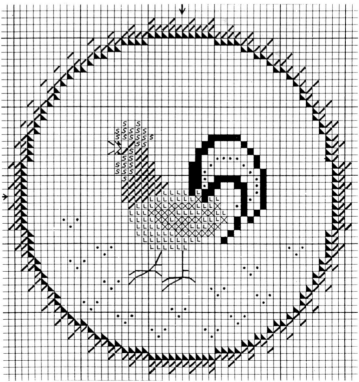

• PLATE LINER WITH CIRCLET OF FLOWERS •

Material: linen, 8 threads per cm.
Cutting size: 16 × 16 cm/6¼ ×
6¼ in.
Finished size: 13 × 13 cm/5 × 5in.
Thread: DMC embroidery floss.
Use 3 strands of floss in the
needle.

Circlet of flowers

☒	972	light orange
⊙	606	dark orange-red
⊞	905	bright avocado

See page 11 for instructions on
completing a round doily.

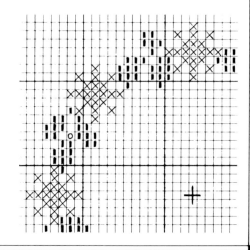

• TABLECLOTH WITH FOLK ART CIRCLE •

Instructions overleaf

TABLECLOTH WITH FOLK ART CIRCLE

Material: light beige Aida,
6 stitches per cm.
Cutting size: 55 × 55 cm/21¾ ×
21¾ in.
Finished size: 50 × 50 cm/19¾ ×
19¾ in.
Thread: DMC embroidery floss.
Use 2 strands of floss in the
needle.

Folk art circle		
N	517	dark cornflower blue
☒	992	medium aqua

See page 11 for instructions on
completing a round tablecloth.

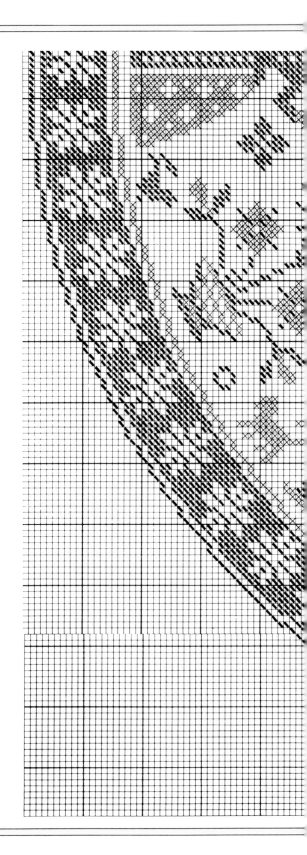

• PLATE LINER WITH HEART WREATH •

Material: linen, 8 threads per cm.
Cutting size: 16 × 16 cm/6¼ × 6¼ in.
Finished size: 13 × 13 cm/5 × 5 in.
Thread: DMC embroidery floss. Use 3 strands of floss in the needle.

Heart wreath

⊠	606	dark orange-red
⫿	904	dark emerald green

See page 11 for instructions on completing a round doily.

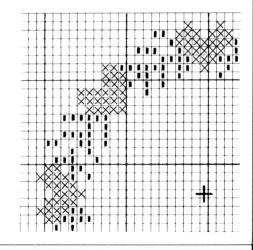

·5·

Squared,
Rectangular and
Allover Designs

Square Designs

• POT HOLDER WITH REINDEER •

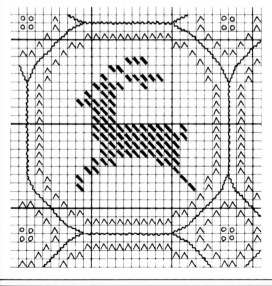

Material: beige Aida, 4½ stitches per cm.

Cutting size: 20 × 20 cm/7¾ × 7¾ in.

Finished size: 17.5 × 17.5 cm/ 7 × 7 in.

Thread: DMC embroidery floss. Use 3 strands of floss in the needle.

Reindeer		
⊙	947	light pumpkin
~	947	light pumpkin (backstitch)
⋀	581	light apple green
◺	433	light chocolate brown

See page 11 for instructions on making a pot holder.

• CENTREPIECE WITH STARS AND HEARTS •

Material: linen, 8 threads per cm.
Cutting size: 40 × 40 cm/15¾ ×
15¾ in.
Finished size: 35 × 35 cm/13¾ ×
13¾ in.
Thread: DMC embroidery floss.
Use 3 strands of floss in the
needle.

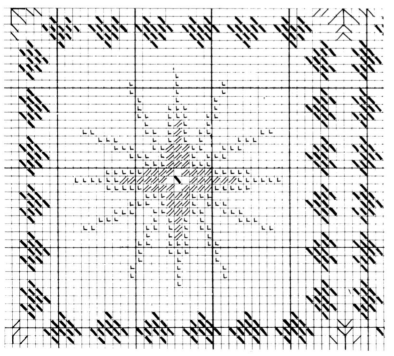

Stars and hearts

L	973	canary yellow
◪	972	light orange
◪	666	scarlet
—	906	medium emerald green (backstitch)

• CHRISTMAS TABLECLOTH •

Material: linen, 10 threads
per cm.
Cutting size: 40 × 40 cm/15¾ ×
15¾ in.
Finished size: 34 × 34 cm/13¼ ×
13¼ in.
Thread: DMC embroidery floss.
Use 2 strands of floss in the
needle.

Hearts in a square

C	725	medium (or metallic) gold
⧄	947	light pumpkin
⊘	606	dark orange-red
●	817	cherry

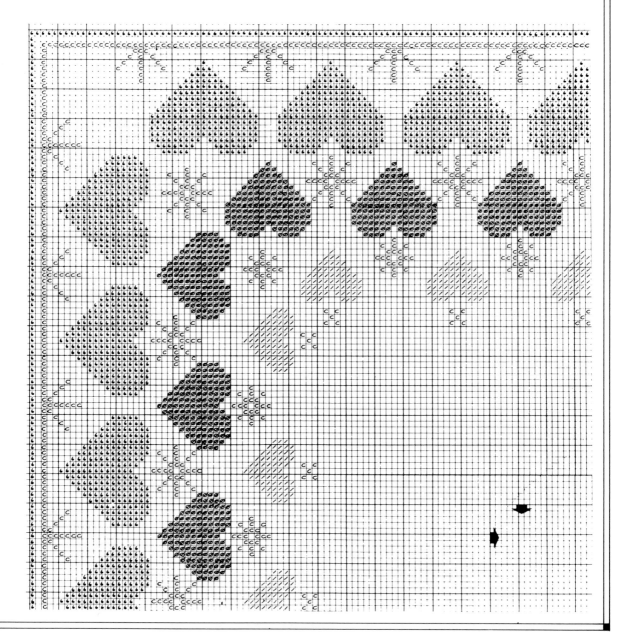

• CENTREPIECE WITH FOLK PEOPLE •

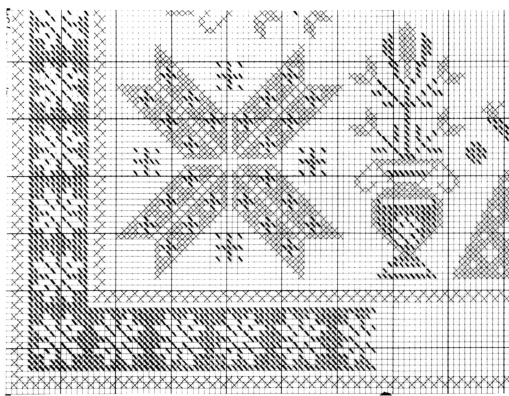

Material: light beige Aida,
6 stitches per cm.
Cutting size: 55 × 55 cm/21¾ ×
21¾ in.
Finished size: 49 × 49 cm/19¼ ×
19¼ in.
Thread: DMC embroidery floss.
Use 2 strands of floss in the
needle.

Folk people
⊠	3328	bright rose
◣	312	dark sky blue

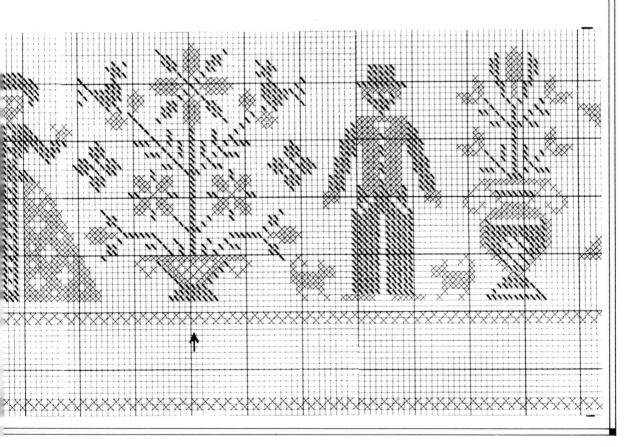

● HOLIDAY CLOTH WITH STAGGERED HEARTS ●

Material: linen, 8 threads per cm.
Cutting size: 33 × 33 cm/13 ×
13 in.
Finished size: 28 × 28 cm/11 ×
11 in.
Thread: DMC embroidery floss.
Use 3 strands of floss in the
needle.

Staggered hearts

---	444	dark yellow (backstitch)
⌃	606	dark orange-red
•	905	bright emerald green

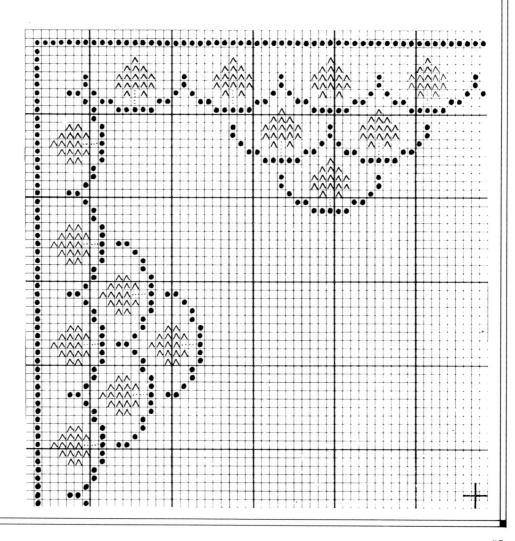

Rectangular Designs

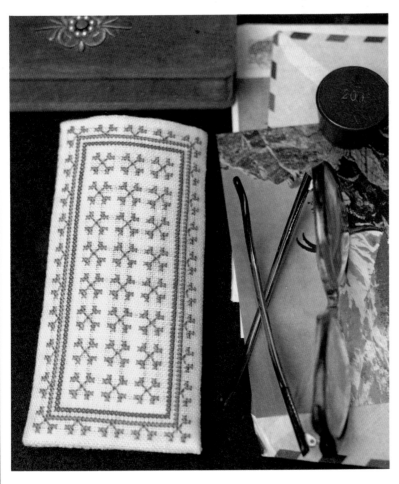

Material: linen, 10 threads per cm.

Cutting size: 2.5 cm/1 in larger than length and width measurements of spectacles.

Backing material: velvet, same size as linen.

Interfacing: 2 pieces, same size as linen.

Thread: DMC embroidery floss. Use 2 strands of floss in the needle.

Criss-cross design

☑	832	dark brass
···	832	dark brass (backstitch)
⊡	920	bright rust
△	989	light grass green

See page 44 for instructions on making a spectacle case.

• SPECTACLE CASE WITH CIRCLES AND CROSSES •

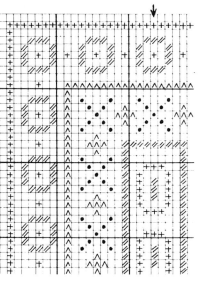

Material: linen, 10 threads per cm.
Cutting size: 2.5 cm/1 in larger than length and width measurements of spectacles.
Backing material: velvet, same size as linen.
Interfacing: 2 pieces, same size as linen.
Thread: DMC embroidery floss. Use 2 strands of floss in the needle.

Circles and crosses

⊞	602	light magenta
⊘	553	medium lilac
⋀	807	light turquoise
⊡	798	dark Dresden blue

See page 44 for instructions on making a spectacle case.

• CHRISTMAS RUNNER WITH GOLDEN STARS •

Material: cotton Aida, 4½ stitches per cm.

Cutting size: 42 × 25 cm/16½ × 9¾ in.

Finished size: 36 × 19 cm/14¼ × 7½ in.

Thread: DMC embroidery floss and golden metallic thread. Use 2 strands of floss in the needle. To add sparkle, mix 1 strand of embroidery floss with 1 of metallic thread.

Golden stars

L	725	medium gold
◣	783	dark gold
•	608	orange-red
⊠	906	medium emerald green

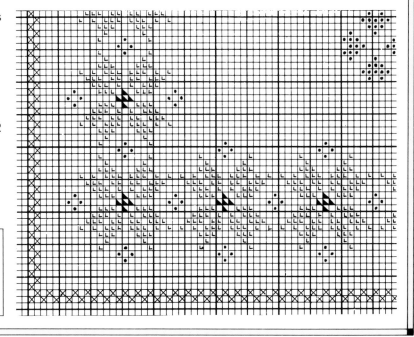

Allover Designs

Material: blue linen, 5 threads per cm.
Cutting size: 22 × 22 cm/8¾ × 8¾ in.
Finished size: 18.5 × 18.5 cm/ 7¼ × 7¼ in.
Thread: DMC embroidery floss. Use 3 strands of floss in the needle.

Swans

L	0000	snow white
•	741	orange
~	741	dark yellow orange (backstitch)
◹	809	light copen blue
∧	907	medium avocado

See page 11 for instructions on making a pot holder.

• CUSHION WITH DUCKS AND DEER •

Material: light beige Aida, 5 stitches per cm.
Cutting size: 40 × 50 cm/15¾ × 19¾ in.
Finished size: 43 × 33 cm/17 × 13 in.

Thread: DMC embroidery floss. Use 2 strands of floss in the needle.

Ducks and deer

⊞	3328	bright rose
●	931	medium soldier blue
⊠	581	light apple green
◣	781	medium coffee

See page 10 for instructions on making a cushion.

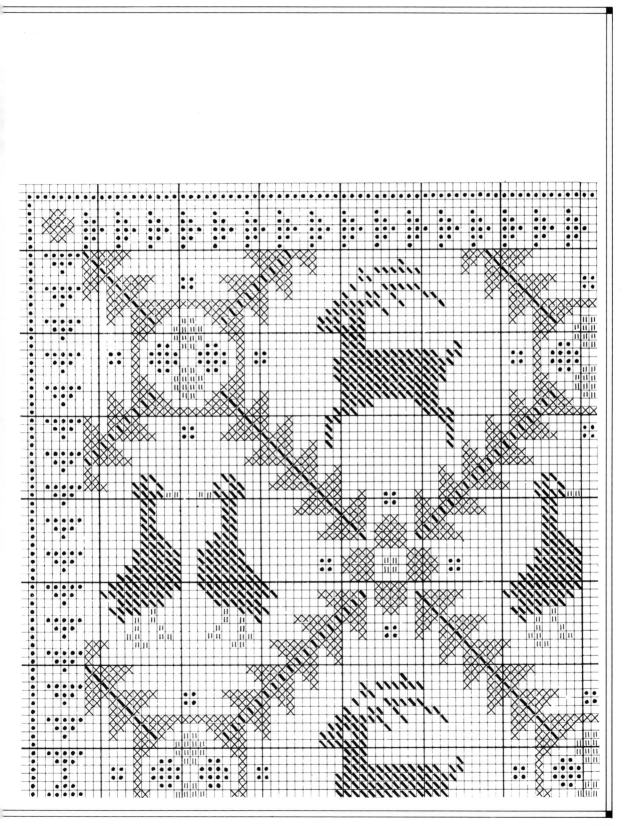

• CHRISTMAS TABLECLOTH WITH •
FLOWERS AND STARS

Material: linen, 8 threads per cm.
Cutting size: 66 × 66 cm/26 ×
26 in.
Finished size: 63 × 63 cm/24 ×
24 in including fringe.
Thread: DMC embroidery floss
and fil or metallic thread. Use 3
strands of floss in the needle; mix
1 strand of metallic thread with 1
strand of 725 floss.

When the embroidery is finished,
make a 2 cm/1 in fringe all
around the edges of the design.

Flowers and stars

⊙	725	medium gold
⊠	676	light mustard (or metallic gold)
⊓	760	medium rose
◪	351	bright peach
◣	349	red-orange
⊡	472	pale avocado
L	471	light avocado

• BOX COVER WITH FLOWERING VINES •

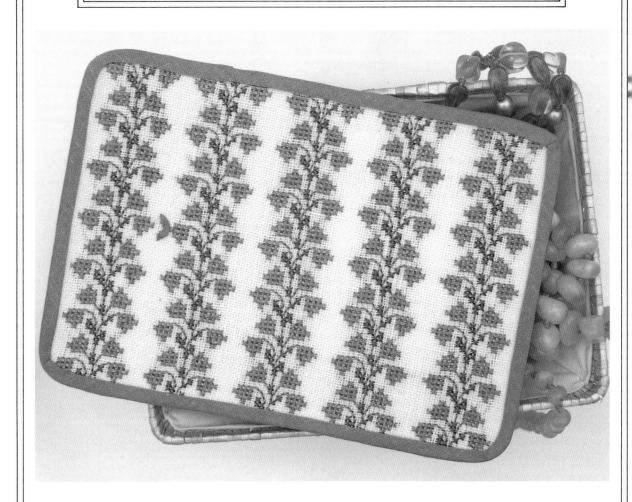

Material: linen, 10 threads per cm.
Cutting size: 20 × 15 cm/7¾ × 6 in.
Finished size: 18½ × 12½ cm/ 7¼ × 5 in.
Thread: DMC embroidery floss. Use 2 strands of floss in the needle.

Flowering vines

●	891	dark coral
⊠	906	medium emerald green
⊟	906	medium emerald green (backstitch)
◣	904	dark emerald green

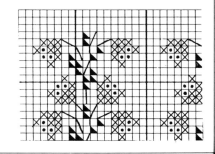

·6·

Large Designs

• CHRISTMAS DECORATION WITH •
SINGING ANGELS

Material: blue linen or burlap,
6 threads per cm.
Cutting size: 45 × 35 cm/17¾ ×
13¾ in.
Finished size: 37 × 29 cm/14½ ×
11½ in.
Thread: DMC embroidery floss.
Use 4 strands of floss in the
needle.

Singing angels

⊡		snow white
⋯		snow white (backstitch)
L	353	light peach
●	726	light (or metallic) gold
—	726	light (or metallic) gold (backstitch)
⊙	973	canary yellow
✕	608	orange-red (and backstitch mouths)
⊓	747	light cornflower blue
◩	703	light Kelly green
◣	420	light acorn

See page 10 for instructions on
making a wallhanging.

• PLACEMAT WITH ASTER •

Materials: linen, 8 threads per cm.
Cutting size: 50 × 40 cm/19¾ ×
15¾ in.
Finished size: 46 × 36 cm/18 ×
14¼ in.
Thread: DMC embroidery floss.
Use 3 strands of floss in the
needle.

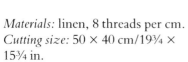

Aster

⬜	725	medium gold
⦁	783	dark gold
·	554	light lilac
⊟	553	medium lilac
◧	552	bright lilac
⊙	732	medium olive
⋀	3053	light sage
◪	3052	medium sage
◤	3051	dark sage

• PLACEMAT WITH ROSES •

Material: linen, 8 threads per cm.
Cutting size: 50 × 40 cm/19¾ ×
15¾ in.
Finished size: 46 × 36 cm/18 ×
14¼ in.
Thread: DMC embroidery floss.
Use 3 strands of floss in the
needle.

Roses

L	776	medium pink
+	894	light coral
N	893	medium coral
•	309	bright carnation pink
○	3012	medium khaki green
I	3348	light spring green
X	3347	medium spring green
Z	3346	dark spring green
◣	3345	hunter green

• WALLHANGING WITH CAT •

Cat

☐		snow white
—		snow white (backstitch)
▨	742	light yellow-orange
⊙	741	medium yellow-orange
⊞	758	light salmon
⊠	907	light emerald green
△	762	pale gray
⊡	318	light gray
⋯	318	light gray (backstitch)
■	310	black
∼	310	black (backstitch)

Material: brown hessian, 6 threads per cm.

Cutting size: 62 × 52 cm/24½ × 20¾ in.

Finished size: 57 × 45 cm/23 × 17¾ in.

Thread: DMC embroidery floss. Use 4 strands of floss in the needle.

See page 10 for instructions on making a wallhanging.

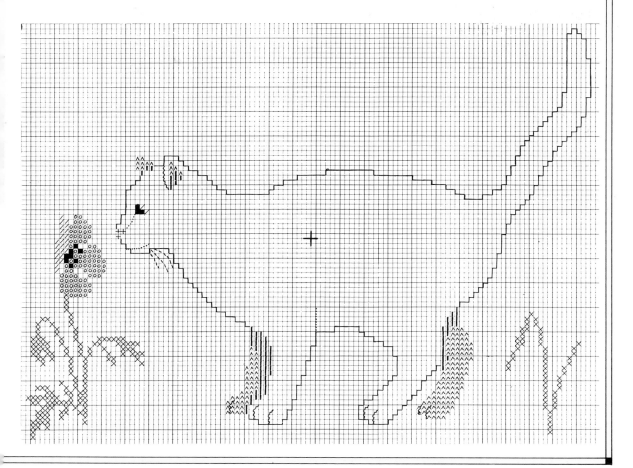

• CHRISTMAS WALLHANGING •

Material: linen, 8 threads per cm.
Cutting size: 26 × 28 cm/10¼ × 11 in.
Finished size: 21 × 23 cm/8¼ × 9 in.
Thread: DMC embroidery floss and fil or gold metallic thread. Use 3 strands of floss in the needle. Mix 1 strand of metallic thread with 1 strand of 725 floss.

Christmas wreath with star

⊡	725	medium and metallic gold
⊡	608	orange-red
⦁	606	dark orange-red
⊡	927	light teal
⋀	502	medium lichen green
⧄	501	bright lichen green
⬛	420	light acorn
...	420	light acorn (backstitch)

See page 10 for instructions on making a wallhanging.

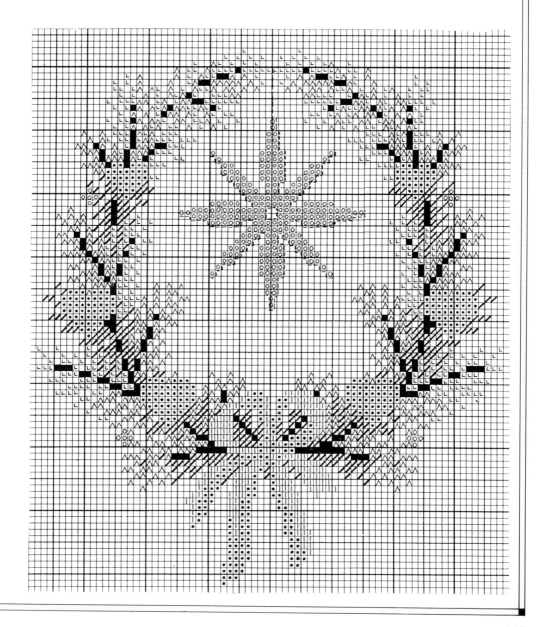

115

• ALPHABET SAMPLER •

Material: red cotton Aida,
4½ stitches per cm.
Cutting size: 35 × 32 cm/13¾ ×
12½ in.
Finished size: 29 × 26 cm/1,1½ ×
10¼ in.
Thread: DMC embroidery floss.
Use 4 strands of floss in the
needle.

Alphabet with figures

☐		snow white
--		snow white (backstitch)
—	445	light yellow (backstitch)
☒	519	medium cornflower blue
⊡	3347	medium spring green
--	3347	medium spring green (backstitch)

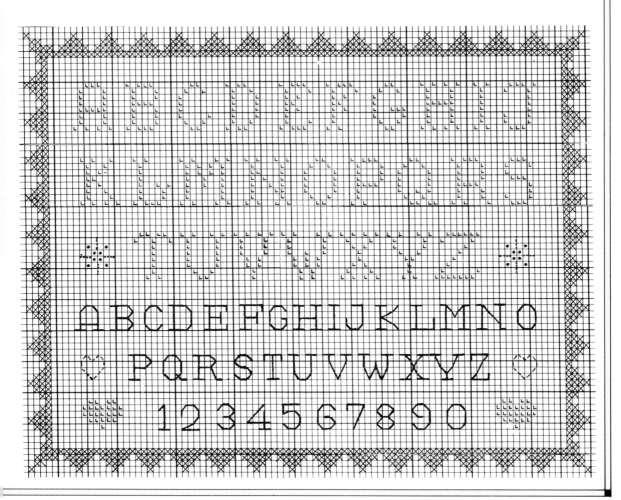

• MEDIEVAL TAPESTRY •

Material: linen, 7 threads per cm.
Cutting size: 65 × 85 cm/25½ ×
33½ in.
Finished size: 54 × 75 cm/21¼ ×
29½ in.
Thread: DMC embroidery floss.
Use 2 strands of floss in the
needle.

Medieval tapestry

C		snow white
☒	950	oatmeal
☐	951	pale buff
T	3078	sunshine yellow
Ø	725	medium gold
◪	783	dark gold
◪	351	bright peach
8	350	dark peach
Z	553	medium lilac
V	794	light marine blue
3	793	medium marine blue
◖	792	bright marine blue
◪	471	light avocado
☒	469	bright avocado
◉	937	deep avocado
⋅	842	light brown
⋎	841	dusty brown
◪	840	medium brown
ℛ	434	dark tan
▶	844	dark slate
●	310	black

See page 10 for instructions on
making a wallhanging.

Instructions overleaf

**MEDIEVAL
TAPESTRY**

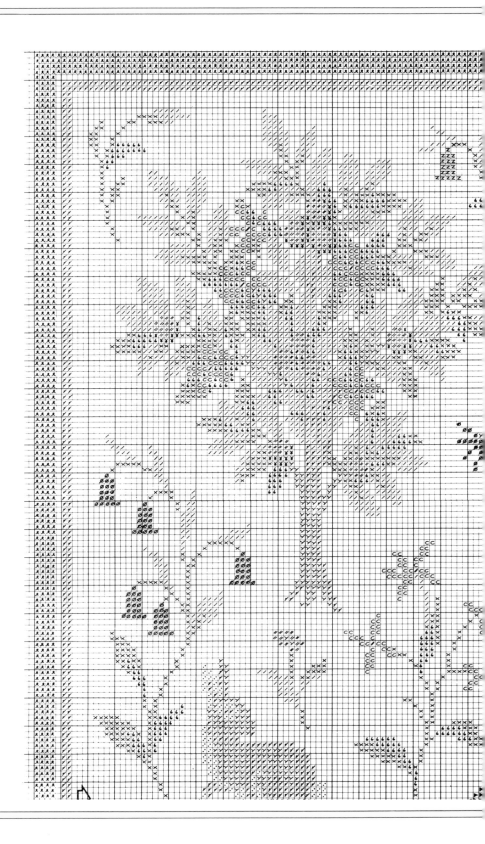

continued overleaf

MEDIEVAL
TAPESTRY

• CURTAIN WITH WILD FLOWERS •

Material: linen, 8 threads per cm.
Cutting size: 45 cm/17¾ in and as
long as required.
Finished size: 40 cm/15¾ in deep.
Thread: DMC embroidery floss.
Use 3 strands of floss in the
needle.

Wild flowers

⊤	307	medium yellow
⊠	444	dark yellow
⊡	972	light orange
Ⓛ	809	medium Dresden blue
◨	793	medium marine blue
■	792	bright marine blue
⊠	471	light avocado
⊞	581	light apple green
◫	580	medium apple green
◪	936	myrtle green
◣	501	bright lichen green
⊟	501	bright lichen green (backstitch)

See page 10 for instructions on
making a curtain.

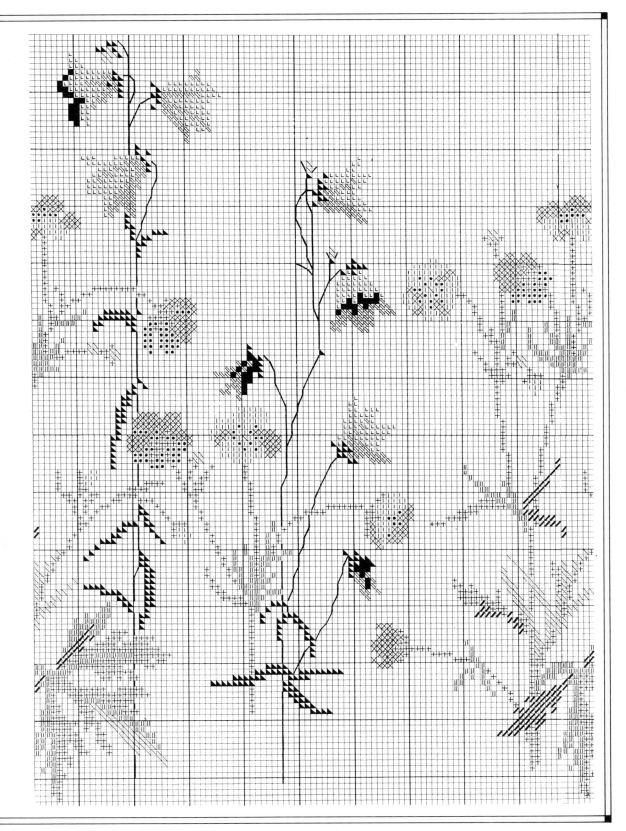

• TABLE RUNNER WITH BLUE FLORID DESIGN •

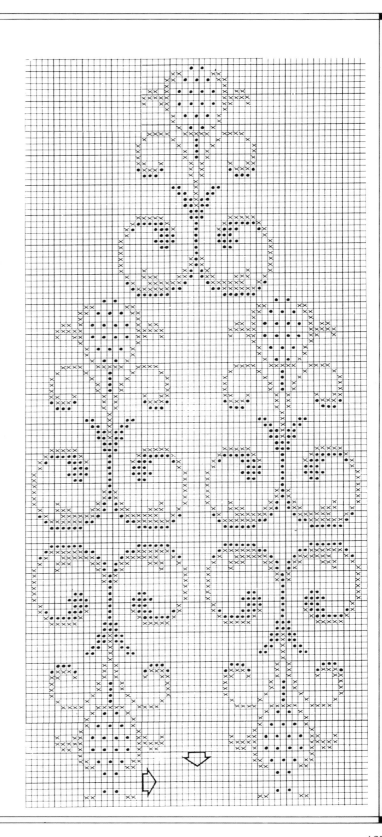

Material: linen, 8 threads per cm.
Cutting size: 22 × 107 cm/8¾ ×
42¼ in.
Finished size: 16 × 102 cm/6¼ ×
40¼ in.
Thread: DMC embroidery floss.
Use 3 strands of floss in the
needle.

Florid design

- 796   bright royal blue
- 798   dark Dresden blue

• CUSHION WITH TWO LADIES •

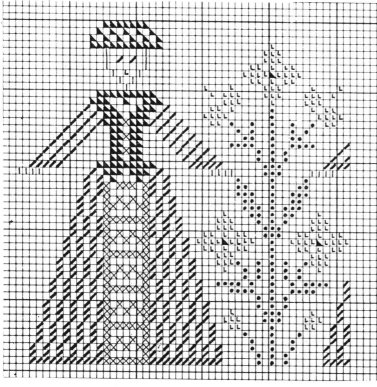

Material: linen, 5 threads per cm.
Cutting size: 2 pieces 45 × 40 cm/
17¾ × 15¾ in.
Finished size: 41 × 36 cm/16¼ ×
14¼ in.
Thread: DMC embroidery floss.
Use 6 strands of floss in the
needle.

Two ladies

⊤	352	medium peach
L	3350	dark dusty pink
⊠	807	light turquoise
▧	797	royal blue
•	580	medium apple green
◣	310	black

See page 10 for instructions on
making a cushion.